The Clutter Book
When You Can't Let Go

The Clutter Book
When You Can't Let Go

Marcie Lovett

Portus Publishing

The Clutter Book: When You Can't Let Go

Copyright ©2011 Marcie Lovett
Organized by Marcie™

Published 2011. All rights reserved. No part of this book may be reproduced, stored in a retrieval system or transmitted in any form or by any means, mechanical, electronic, photocopying, recording or otherwise, without written permission from the publisher.

Cover design by Robyn Shrater Seemann

Author photograph ©SimplyMui Photography

ISBN-13: 978-0615483726
ISBN-10: 0615483720

Printed in the United States of America by CreateSpace.

Published by Portus Publishing.

For information about special discounts for bulk purchases, please contact sales@organizedbymarcie.com.

This book contains the author's opinions and professional experience based on her work as a Professional Organizer and Productivity Consultant. Mention of specific companies, organizations or authorities in this book does not imply endorsement by the publisher, nor does mention of specific companies, organizations or authorities imply that they endorse this book. At the time this book was published, all Web sites were accurate.

Table of Contents

Living with Clutter 1
Get Ready to Let Go 17
Goal Setting 18
Creating Systems 21

When You Can't Let Go of Shopping 30
Shopping as Recreation 34
Bargain Hunting 35

When You Can't Let Go of Clothing 39

When You Can't Let Go of Projects 43

When You Can't Let Go of Paper 45
Creating a Paper Management System 47
Mail, Newspapers, Newsletters, Magazines, Catalogs 52
Filing 54
Organizing Your Work Space 62

When You Can't Let Go of Technophobia 67
Using Technology 68
When You Can't Let Go of Email 71

When You Can't Let Go of Sentiment 77
Collections 80

When You Can't Let Go of Habits 85
Value Your Time 88
Commitments 90
Productivity 91
Attention/Distraction 94

Multitasking 96
Procrastination 98
Perfection 103
Decision Making 104
Data Gathering 106
Crisis Mode 108

Living Your Plan 111

About Hoarding 113

Resources 114

Introduction

I have been a Professional Organizer and Productivity Consultant for several years and before that I shared ideas informally with people about organizing their spaces. I didn't realize that other people didn't have the same skills that I had when it came to sorting, grouping and eliminating clutter.

For the past few years, I have been thinking differently about my profession. As a group, organizers tend to promote living with less. Although I endorse a "simple living" approach, I now recognize that doesn't work with everyone. So the aim of this book is to help you learn to live with what you have. If you choose to be surrounded by stuff, we'll come up with a plan to make you comfortable.

After speaking to groups, participants would ask if I had written a book. My standard reply was, "There are so many organizing books already and I don't want to add to people's book clutter." I have seen people's collections of organizing books, purchased with the hope that they will initiate changes. Buying a book, however, will not create the change you want. Participating actively in the process will make the difference.

That is why I wrote this book. I will ask you questions and urge you to look at your relationships with things. In addition, I aim to inspire you to think about how you live your life and what you want to change.

If you don't want to change, that's okay, too. In that case, I hope to encourage you to enjoy your life and your choices.

Living with Clutter

What happened?

Clutter usually builds up gradually without your realizing that it's happening. One day you find that you can't open a door or move easily through a hallway or find what you're looking for because there's too much stuff. It got that way because you weren't paying attention. Now that you've noticed, you can do something about it, but first you have to believe that you can live differently and that your time and effort are worth spending on creating the change.

Everyone has things come into their homes: paper, clothing, furniture, household goods, books, etc. Once things are in your house, either they become valued or they create clutter.

If you value something, you take good care of it by using it and storing it properly. Not everyone values the same things. Some people put a monetary value on items; others may highly value things that have sentimental meaning to them. You may also find that the things you value change over time.

Exercise 1 – What you value

List three things in your home that you value highly, along with the reason why each is valuable to you. It might be due to the person who gave it to you or where you acquired it or because you paid a lot of money for it. Be specific about the reason.

Item #1 _____

Reason _____

Item #2 _____

Reason _____

Item #3 _____

Reason _____

Were you able to complete the exercise quickly or did you agonize over it? Are you surprised by your choices? People typically assign value to things for one of two reasons: cost or sentimentality.

Where are the things that you listed in *Exercise 1*? If you can't find them or you can't get to them because they're buried beneath other things, you are not valuing them. Things you truly value should be treated with respect. Organizing expert Peter Walsh emphasizes the need to "honor" the things you value. That means taking them out and washing, dusting or polishing them and putting them where they can be used and enjoyed. Moldering boxes of unknown items are not being honored.

If one of the items on your list is a piece of furniture, for example, put it in a room where you can see it regularly and use it properly. If it is a book, put it in a bookcase or on a shelf where you can reach it and refer to it whenever you like. Display delicate objects in a safe place if you are afraid they will get ruined. Wrap seasonal items protectively and store them to avoid damage until you display them again.

> From the moment of birth we are immersed in action, and can only fitfully guide it by taking thought.
> - Alfred North Whitehead

The amount of time you spend focusing on the three things in *Exercise 1* will depend upon the size of each piece and how difficult it is to reach. You may be able to finish in an afternoon or it might take several weeks. Stick with it, as long as it takes, it will be worth the effort.

After you identify the items on your list and show them the respect they deserve, consider how good it feels to enjoy the things you treasure. There is more work to do and the positive feelings might drift away when you have to dig back in to the clutter. Revisit your success when you feel discouraged.

You may be faced with the things you took out of a piece of furniture or the things you had to move to get to an object on your list. Don't just dump them in a convenient place; you'll simply have to deal with them some other time. In the next section, we will create a plan for tackling the clutter. Until then, put everything in a box or an isolated section of the room so you will be ready to continue.

Being organized is just being thoughtful. Put some thought into what you're going to do, where you're going to put things, what you need to accomplish. Thinking about your tasks instead of moving on autopilot changes your perspective.

It took time for your clutter to accumulate; it will take time to move through it. Don't rush through the process. When you keep the end result in mind, you will be more motivated to continue.

Exercise 2 – Keep the end in mind

What are the results you want? Describe how your home, office, time, finances or relationships would look when you let go of the clutter that is holding you back.

_____

_____

_____

_____

People tell me stories about their clutter and how it affects them. Here are some of the reasons they have given for wanting to let go of it:

- I want to simplify my life and keep what has meaning and importance to me.
- I want to experience peace of mind.
- I want to save time instead of spending it looking for things.
- I want to experience a sense of calm and have less stress.
- I want to have pride in my home and feel joy in having guests over.
- I want to have less family tension.
- I want greater efficiency in my office.
- I want to eliminate late fees for bills.
- I want to have more time for the things that are important to me and spend less time doing things I don't care about.
- I want to be able to relax without being swamped by lists of things I need to do at work and at home.

You may have some of the same concerns.

What do I do now?

Now it's time to make some decisions about your stuff and your space. Throw away things that are broken or unusable so they don't take up room you could use for something else. If you've been holding onto an object because you want to fix it, set a specific time frame for the repair. Write it in your calendar as an appointment. If you haven't fixed it yourself or taken it to be repaired by the deadline, it's time to let it go.

If you are holding onto things because you think they will be useful to someone you know, give them to that person. If you find out that he or she isn't interested in the items, don't be offended. Most people already have plenty of their own stuff and might be trying to break the habit of bringing in more.

Many people hold onto things because they want to have a yard sale. I think yard sales are a lot of work for little return; however, if you want to have one, choose a place to set aside everything you want to sell and commit to a date. Once you mark the date on your calendar, you are more likely to follow through. If you change your mind, you can donate everything you have gathered.

You may have clutter that doesn't belong to you. In that case, let the owner know that you are making room in your home and that the things need to be picked up by a specific date. If they are not retrieved, you reserve the right to get rid of them. Don't allow yourself to become a storage facility for other people's things.

Clutter affects your mood. Take a look around your home or office and think about how it makes you feel. If you feel good about it, great! When you feel surrounded by disorder, though, it affects you negatively. Clutter causes stress and removing clutter helps relieve stress.

If you are starting to feel anxious about the possibility of getting rid of your clutter, keep reading. No one is going to force you to get rid of anything. Organizing is not about throwing everything out, but about finding appropriate places for the things you value. What you keep will be determined by the amount of space you have and the amount of time you want to spend maintaining your belongings.

Start with one manageable area and create a vision for it. Think about how you want to use the space, how it will look and how you will feel being in there. Be realistic; nobody can live in a magazine-perfect house, but your home can still feel "lived in" without being cluttered. If you like to be surrounded by reminders of good times, you should keep those things in view. Don't, however, confuse those reminders with stacks of mail, books and magazines that you haven't paid attention to, along with other things you haven't made decisions about. Clutter is stuff that gets in your way; things that you like to be surrounded with add value to your life.

> ## The reason to let go of clutter is to remove obstacles

Are you holding onto things that have no meaning or value to you anymore? If so, someone else could benefit from them. Would you feel better letting go of something if you knew that it could be valuable to someone else?

People often get stuck, worrying about where their possessions are going to end up. I respectfully suggest that no matter who gets them, you will be better off not having them hanging around your house, keeping you from achieving your goals. Everything you discard will end up with just the right person, even if it isn't someone you know.

You can donate to charity just about anything you have that is unwanted but still functional. This serves multiple purposes: you have less clutter, you could take a tax deduction and someone else ends up with something he or she needs.

There are charities that sell donations to raise money for their programs and charities that give donated goods directly to end users. Where you donate your things will depend upon what you have to give and whether you feel strongly about a particular cause.

I will caution you that it is important not to let the donation process keep you from moving forward. Some people get so caught up in finding the "perfect" recipient for each thing that they're unable to donate anything at all. Concentrate on how much better you will feel when you aren't weighed down by things you don't need, regardless of who ends up with them.

Once you let go of the clutter, chances are very good that you won't miss it. In addition, you will realize how much room it took up in your physical and mental space.

Some things may not be worth donating; if it's not good enough to give to a friend, it's probably not good enough to give to charity, either. In that case, the best thing to do is throw it away.

In order to be successful at keeping your space clear, you have to change the way you think. Just like any other positive habit you want to develop, it will take time and effort. Don't expect to make huge changes suddenly; the best changes are those you introduce over time and maintain as routines.

> Motivation is what gets you started. Habit is what keeps you going. —Jim Ryun

If you have ever tried to lose weight, you know that you can't expect to lose 20 pounds overnight. View losing clutter the same way. You could go on a clutter "crash diet" and dump everything you have, but you wouldn't learn the behaviors that will help you maintain your new lifestyle. Chances are, like going on a crash diet to lose weight, you would return to your old habits and start letting clutter back into your life.

The first step to changing your habits is changing the way you think about yourself. Instead of calling yourself lazy, careless or sloppy, substitute one of these messages: I care about my property. I take the time to put things away. I spend money wisely. I understand that my belongings don't define me.

Exercise 3 – Express yourself

Create your own message that defines the way you want to feel about your relationship with your things:

_____

_____

_____

_____

_____

Substitute the message you wrote, above, anytime you begin to think negatively about yourself and your clutter. By changing the way you think, you can change your beliefs, which leads to creating habits. You will learn more about changing your habits in upcoming chapters.

Recently I have been questioning the whole concept of "organizing" and what it means to "be organized." When people find out what I do, they often tell me that they aren't organized and never will be. So what? It's nothing to be ashamed of. If someone hasn't taught you the skills, you can't be faulted for not knowing how to do something. I believe that everyone can learn to improve their environment and their productivity by letting go of clutter. If you can't let go, you can learn how to manage your clutter so that you can get the most out of your spaces and your time.

The thought of having to tackle many years' worth of accumulation can keep you from even starting the process. Putting aside the fear of confronting all that stuff may be hard, but you can do it.

I created the **ESP** system, have used it for years and find that it works well for clients who are ready to let go of clutter. The way to be successful is to start small.

Empty the area – take everything out

Sort the contents into three categories – keep, toss or donate

Place – put things that you value in a logical location

Whether this is your 1st or your 50th attempt at letting go of clutter, this time you are going to experience success by starting with a small project. People get frustrated when they take on too much and can't finish right away. You will not realistically be able to declutter a garage or a basement in two hours, for example. Be reasonable about what you expect to accomplish.

Define your area as a drawer, a shelf, a corner of a room or a section of a closet. It might feel like you will never finish your project if you have to work on such small spaces, but you will. Remember, if you do a little at a time, you will gradually notice the change. If you don't do anything, nothing will change.

Start with whatever is easiest to get to. Removing larger pieces first will make your piles decrease more quickly and you'll be motivated by the progress you've made.

Empty the area (drawer, shelf or corner) of everything. Put all the stuff on a flat surface, so you can see it and make decisions about it. Wipe down the area so that when you put things back, it will be clean and clear. This is not the time to deep-clean the entire room; concentrate on the limited area you chose and don't spend all your time on cleaning in order to avoid decision making.

Sorting the things you have and making decisions about it all is challenging for most people. Although it might be difficult for you, try to put aside the sentiment and don't think about how much you paid for things. If you are having trouble deciding whether to keep something, don't talk yourself into it.

Most of my clients find **S**orting to be painful, which is why they don't get started. Rather than thinking of it as an endless, exhausting task, consider what your space will look like when you have less to put away, store, move, dust, vacuum, sweep, clean, polish and insure. Instead of spending your time cleaning and maintaining your stuff (or paying someone else to do it), you will have time and money to spend on the people and activities that you enjoy.

At this point, you only have to make one choice about each thing: keep it, donate it, throw it out or recycle it.

You have permission to let go of things that don't fit in your life

I have found that a lot of people feel they need permission to let go of things, especially when those things were given as gifts or belonged to a loved one. Letting go of those things can cause feelings of guilt or betrayal. Ask yourself if the person who gave it to you would really want you to keep something that you no longer need, want or enjoy. I believe that if the person truly cared about you, he or she would want you to let go of what you can't use and allow someone else to benefit from it. You will learn more about letting go of sentimental attachments later in the book.

Paul Graham, a computer programmer and writer, has a very healthy perspective about "stuff." In an essay, he noted, "The only way you're ever going to extract any value from [your stuff] is to use it. And if you don't have any immediate use for it, you probably never will." Coming from someone who is not an organizer, the message is very powerful.

People are reluctant to part with things that they (or someone else) spent a lot of money on. Keeping something because it cost a lot of money doesn't bring the money back.

Just because something cost a lot of money doesn't make it valuable. Neither does age. People hold onto things thinking that they will sell them at some undetermined time in the future and make a lot of money. If you have a collection of items you are hoping to sell for a profit, keep in mind that most "limited-edition collectibles" do not increase in value. They are mass-produced and appeal to a limited audience.

Would you still keep it if it hadn't cost anything? Is it really the item you are keeping or the feelings about how the money was spent? Whether it was a bargain or a budget buster is not important. If you don't love it and don't use it, it doesn't matter how much it cost; it's just taking up space.

You may think that because you already own something, it isn't costing you anything. But it is. It's costing you time to clean it or maintain it. It's costing you peace of mind. It's costing you space that could be used for something else. And if you're paying for storage because you've run out of room, it is costing you rent every month.

You might be hesitant to let go of something because you paid a lot for it and you haven't used it yet. Whether it doesn't fit, doesn't go with anything or doesn't appeal to you anymore, don't hang on to it. If you have no use for something, you aren't helping yourself by keeping it around in case you change your mind.

Take money out of the equation

If you no longer have a need for an item, let it go. If it can be used by someone else, give it away. If it is too worn to be useful to anyone else, throw it away. If you want to invest the time and energy, you can try to sell it.

When you sell something, don't expect to get back the amount of money that the item cost when it was new. A woman in one of my workshops spoke about selling everything from her late in-laws' home, including a very expensive adjustable bed that sold for only $25 at the estate sale. To the buyer, it was just used furniture.

People often tell me that they aren't using something, but they can't let it go because they are saving it. They may be saving something for future children or grandchildren, for when they lose a few pounds, for when they find time to pursue a hobby, or because it's just too nice to use.

Instead of saving things for some magical time when you might be ready to use them, seriously consider whether holding onto them improves your life. I have seen scores of homes with brand-new items tucked away because the owner was saving them. Don't save things for later; use them now, enjoy them now.

Enjoy it now or let it go

When you're **S**orting, look at the number of things you have. How many pairs of black pants do you really need? Unless you have a job where you wear the same thing every day, it doesn't make sense to "stock up" on black pants or white shirts or navy shoes or any other clothing. By owning less, you can buy something new when the style or your taste changes.

If you have multiple casserole dishes or serving trays or coffee cups because you used to entertain a lot, consider how many are reasonable for you to keep and let go of the rest. Look at how you live now and keep only what fits in your life.

Clutter often is the result of delayed decisions. When you put off decision making, you actually are making a choice by choosing to do nothing about it. You are allowing the details of your life to overwhelm you when you don't act on them.

As you **S**ort, you will determine what you want to keep before you put anything away. Take into account the amount of space you have, as well as your lifestyle and routines. Also consider the amount of time you want to devote to maintaining your things. To help you decide what stays, ask yourself the following questions and be realistic when you answer:

- Have you used it recently?
- Do you have something like it?
- Will you remember you have it?
- Will you be able to find it?
- Does it get in the way of finding something else you need to use?
- Can it be replaced easily?
- Can you borrow one from someone else?
- What's the worst that can happen if you let it go?

Now it's time to find a **P**lace for everything you want to keep. The most sensible solution is to put things where you use them. If you have a dog, keep the leash near the door. If you collect coupons, keep them in your car. If you do crafts in the dining room, choose a spot where you can leave materials and projects when you're not working on them.

Everything you own needs a home

There is no "right place" to keep things. What's "right" is what works for you, because you need to find things and put them back when you're finished with them. Think about how and where you use things. For example, you might keep one pair of scissors in the bathroom, one in the kitchen and one in your desk. Someone else might keep one in the bedroom, one in the family room and one in the garage. Make sure you are able to return things to their homes or you will end up buying more to replace the ones that you can't find because they are scattered around.

I have clients who have collections of bags of miscellaneous stuff because they were having company over and they cleared the entertaining areas. They throw everything into bags, then toss them into a closet or spare room. Afterward, no one remembers to go back and get the bags. Meanwhile, invitations are lost, bills go unpaid and duplicates are purchased because they've disappeared into a corner of a closet.

Don't put it down, put it away

Putting things in containers isn't a better solution, unless you use them intentionally. You can buy baskets and boxes and bins that allow you to hide stuff and give you the illusion that you've cleared away clutter, when all you've done is stashed it out of sight. If you shove into containers anything that's lying around, you won't be able to find things when you need them. Instead, group like items and put the containers where you can find them.

Although it may be tempting, don't buy containers before you see what you have to put inside them. I recommend buying multiples of the same size container so you can stack them easily once they're filled. If you are grouping toiletries and healthcare items, for example, they usually fit nicely into shoebox-size containers that can be stored in the linen closet or under a bathroom sink. In a garage or basement, you probably will need large totes to store tools, sporting goods or other seasonal items.

Gather together all the things that belong in your selected space, and put them back. You can use dividers to split up the space or containers to hold small items. Don't stack things so high that they will topple over or risk tumbling down if you take out the lowest one. Be aware of how far you can reach; put your most-used items in the area between your shoulders and your waist, so you can access them easily. If you can't find a place for something after you have put everything else away, consider whether you need it.

What about the rest of it?

You find personal grooming implements in the dining room and bills in the bedroom. Clients often tell me that they put things down to take care of "later" instead of putting them away right away. When you don't make time to address these issues, "later" never comes and clutter builds up as a result of unmade decisions.

When you are unable to put things away immediately, use the "get close" premise. It may not always be convenient to stop what you're doing and take care of something at that moment, so put it close to where it needs to go. For example, if you are upstairs and you don't want to interrupt what you're doing to return something to a downstairs room, place it at the top of the stairs and take it with you the next time you go down. If you want to put something in the car, set it near the door to go out.

Don't be a dumper

What you don't want to do, however, is start making piles that linger for weeks. You need to move the things to their intended homes when you finish what you were doing. When you take a moment to put things away now, you avoid hours of cleaning up later. As productivity expert David Allen says, "If you can do it in two minutes or less, do it now."

Grouping tasks will allow you to use your time wisely. Otherwise, you might be likely to flit from room to room, not completing anything. This is especially important if you are easily distracted; you find yourself dashing from project to project because you get sidetracked when you leave the room to put something away.

You will be more productive if you stay where you are and finish what you are doing; then put everything away when you complete the task. Put a little extra thought into your actions, instead of letting things fall where you drop them.

> *We cannot become what we need to be by remaining what we are.* — Max Du Pree

If you don't have enough space to keep everything you want, you might be considering or already be paying for outside storage. If you are selling your home and need it to show better, putting your things in storage is a good idea. Likewise, if you are between homes and need a place to keep your things, self-storage units are great. However, more and more people are using storage units as a way to avoid making decisions about their excess belongings.

There also are lots of people who save things because they think they will be "worth something someday." Is the cost to rent a storage unit worth the gamble that the items will increase in value?

If you have things in storage, consider how much that storage costs you each month and what the stored objects are worth. Could you replace them with the money you spent holding onto them? Take inventory of what you are storing and decide whether you're spending your money wisely.

Get Ready to Let Go

Lots of my clients have large pockets of clutter in otherwise well-organized homes. They create "dumping grounds" for papers and incomplete projects and never deal with them. Clutter often builds up gradually without your even noticing, until it grows out of control.

People are amazed that they have lived for months or years with stuff they didn't need and that a few hours spent decluttering can make a big difference in their environments. Once they let go of the clutter, they realize how much space it took up and how it influenced their outlooks.

If you don't know where to start, here is a list of things that you should be able to let go of easily:

- Anything that is soiled, broken, damaged or torn beyond repair
- Anything that is missing pieces that can't be replaced
- Anything that is a duplicate of something you don't use often
- Anything that contains outdated information
- Anything that doesn't matter to you anymore
- Anything that makes you unhappy to see it

During the **S**orting process, you asked yourself questions about the objects you considered keeping. If you still can't decide whether to keep something, here are some more questions:

- Is it worth the time and effort to maintain it?
- If you were moving, would you pay to take it with you?
- Would you buy it again?
- Are you still interested in it?
- Do you have a specific place to keep it?

If you answer "yes" to any of the questions, then you should keep the item. If you can't come up with even one good reason to keep it, let it go. Don't talk yourself into keeping something that doesn't bring you pleasure.

Goal Setting

Before you start any project, you need to have a goal in mind. If you say that your goal is "get organized," you really haven't set a goal at all. In order to be successful, you need to decide exactly what you want to accomplish, how you will do it, and when. Otherwise, what you think is a goal is just an idea.

My realization came when I heard someone give a speech on the difference between goals and dreams. A dream, she said, is something you think about and hope for, while a goal is something you work actively to accomplish. Whether your goal is to lose weight, get fit, gain knowledge or organize your space, you have to work at achieving it.

> It must be borne in mind that the tragedy of life does not lie in not reaching your goal. The tragedy of life lies in having no goal to reach.
> – Benjamin Mays

If you compare letting go of clutter to weight loss, it would be comparable to saying "My goal is to lose weight." If you really want to lose weight, you need to decide how many pounds you will lose, in what period of time, and what you are going to do to change your eating and exercise habits. In other words, you need to come up with a plan.

George T. Doran is credited with developing the SMART acronym for clearly defining goal setting. Following this plan will provide structure and support for identifying your goals and will allow you to evaluate the skills and strategies necessary to accomplish them.

Using the first letters of each of the following words, Mr. Doran came up with **SMART**:

> **S**pecific
>
> **M**easurable
>
> **A**chievable
>
> **R**ealistic
>
> **T**imely

Choose the project you are going to start with: a closet, a room or piece of furniture, for example. Be **S**pecific.

Break your task up into **M**easurable steps. You want to be able to determine your success.

In order to complete your project, you need to have all the materials and skills necessary to do the work. Gather tools and supplies so you don't have to stop in the middle of the job. If you don't have the physical ability or knowledge to make the goal **A**chievable, you might need to hire someone or ask for help. If you need someone else to help you, make sure that person is committed to the time frame you scheduled.

If you don't have the time, money or ability to complete the project right now, reconsider the goal. Can you make it smaller? Go with a less expensive option? Schedule it for a time when you don't have other obligations? Be **R**ealistic.

Taking into account all of the rest of your responsibilities, decide how much **T**ime you are able to devote to this project, which day(s) you will work on it and when you will finish.

Here is an example:

> I will empty the kitchen pantry and get rid of any food that is past its expiration date or that we don't like. I will put open packages into canisters or plastic containers and group them by type of food. I will complete one shelf each night, after dinner and before the TV show I like to watch.

In addition to being **S**pecific, **M**easurable and **T**imely, this goal is **A**chievable and **R**ealistic. In order to reach the goal, you would need to have the containers on hand and commit to being available during the time you planned to work.

Exercise 4 – Be objective

Create your **SMART** goal here:

Specific _____

_____

Measurable _____

_____

Achievable _____

_____

Realistic _____

_____

Timely _____

_____

Now that you've decided what, when and how you're going to start, you need to schedule the steps to make them happen. Mark appointments on your calendar to complete the job. Break them up into smaller assignments if it is a large job. If you need to ask someone to help you or do some preparation before you can do your part, get that person scheduled in advance.

Creating Systems

Everyone needs systems to keep track of the things and information in their lives. There are lots of systems that already exist, so you don't have to create your own. People continue to live with clutter because they say that they haven't found the right system. Don't wait to find the perfect system, just start with something to keep the details of your life from overwhelming you.

To start letting go of clutter, you need a system for collecting appointments, tasks and ideas. Many people are overwhelmed by all the choices available: paper or electronic, pocket-size or large-format, daily or weekly. I have found that people seem to think that the more complicated a system is, the better it will work, when the opposite is true. I suggest starting simply. You don't want to invest a lot of money in a planning device when you're not sure that you're going to keep up with it.

Small steps lead to great accomplishments

The easiest, cheapest, most portable tool is a pad of paper or notebook, where you can record phone messages, things you need to do, places you need to go, etc. Choose something that's small enough that you can carry around with you, but not so small that you will misplace it easily.

If you have had success in the past with a paper planner, there are many products you can buy, which vary in price and complexity. To make the investment pay off, you have to commit to using your planner consistently. If you continue to scribble notes on scraps of paper and stuff them into your planner, you will not be using it effectively. The way to stop losing things and missing appointments is to write everything down in one place.

Some people believe that they should have separate business and personal calendars, but that doesn't always work. You don't want to cancel a meeting with a client because you forgot you had a dentist appointment scheduled for the same time. You might benefit from using different colors to distinguish personal from business activities, but don't overdo it or you won't be able to maintain the system.

> ### Letting Go, Real Life:
>
> I keep one running list of everything I have to do, or want to do, not including my routine tasks. If you looked at my list right now, you'd see "Buy carpet" and "Call painters for estimates," among other things. Each day I look at the list and see what I can transfer to that day or the next few days. Once everything on the list is crossed out, I toss the page.
>
> When I think of something while I'm in the middle of doing something else, I add it to the list. I am able to "dump" my thoughts in one place: off my mind and onto the list. I don't have to think about all the dozens of things that have to be done, which frees me to complete the activities I've chosen to work on that day.
>
> While none of the things on my list keeps me up at night, they do take up space in my brain that could be used for other things. This system works well and keeps projects moving forward.

If you prefer to use an electronic system, you can create simple lists in your word-processing program. When you've accomplished tasks, you can delete or strike through them. There is something very satisfying about seeing a list of things with lines through them, knowing you completed them all. If you have a calendar program, utilize the task list, which you can view as part of your daily calendar. You can create separate sections for phone calls, errands and other tasks. If you use a hand-held device, put a daily appointment on your calendar to remind you to sync to your computer so you don't lose vital information.

Once you choose a system for containing your thoughts, ideas and actions, use it for at least 21 days in a row. Studies show that three weeks of daily effort can turn a new practice into habit. People tend to give up before the three-week period is over and say that the system didn't work. If, after three weeks of really being aware of your new system and using it every day, you still feel like it isn't going to work for you, try something else. Don't give up on it just because it's hard; you need to be determined to make this change.

When you are comfortable using your idea-collection system, you can move on to creating systems for handling the physical clutter around you.

Right now, this may seem like an overwhelming commitment of time and energy. In reality, the system you choose is simply a set of ideas or procedures that allows you to get through your day more successfully. I also refer to them as rules, parameters, boundaries, guidelines or methods.

Some rules are determined for you: The day your trash or recycling is collected, the time you need to be at work, the amount of room you have in a cabinet, for example. There are consequences when you don't abide by these parameters. When you set up your own guidelines for a behavior, you decide what is important, but you also need to establish what the consequences will be if you don't follow through.

Systems, alone, will not fix a clutter problem. A lot of people are constantly looking for a better system to restore order to their lives. Your commitment to the "rules" is going to determine your success. If you believe that a new system isn't going to work for you, you're right. In order for any process to work, you must be willing to change your habits and be thoughtful about the way you do things from now on.

The most important thing to remember is that organizing systems don't need to be complicated; keep yours simple and you will be more likely to use it. You don't need to spend a lot of money on products, either; use what you already have. If you need to buy containers, you can start out at discount department stores.

Consider how and where you're going to use bins or baskets before you buy them; don't buy something just because you like the way it looks or it seems like it might be useful somewhere. You also need to measure the things they will hold and the area they will occupy; otherwise, you risk ending up with container clutter.

After you group items during the **S**orting phase, look at how many of each thing you have. If you have more than you need, consider giving away the ones you don't use. You might find that you have four ice-cream scoops and you really only need two. Pick the two you like best and put the others in your donation bin. Look critically at each group and be honest about your needs.

> It doesn't matter how slowly you go so long as you do not stop. — Confucius

Before you **P**lace the things you decide to keep, you need to categorize them. You might use size or color or function. I like to alphabetize things. If I didn't alphabetize my CDs, I'd never know what I had or where a particular one was. Some of my clients separate their spices by cooking and baking. Others divide their closets into work and casual clothes. I even have clients who shelve their books by the Dewey Decimal System! The key is to use what works for you. Your system is going to enable you to find things quickly and put them away easily. It will take a little planning and time to set up, but when you continue to apply the rule, it will become habit.

Probably the easiest way to create a new routine is to "hook" a behavior to something you already do. You might be practicing this technique already: When you change your clocks to accommodate Daylight Saving Time, you change the batteries in your smoke detectors. When you are ready to go to bed, you brush your teeth. When you fill up your car's gas tank, you clean the windshield.

If you want to create a system for doing laundry, you could hook it to watching TV in the evening. Start by putting laundry in the washing machine before you eat dinner. When you finish eating, put it in the dryer and take it out of the dryer before you sit down to watch TV.

While you watch TV, fold it and, during a commercial, put it away. Once you start to do this every day, you will have developed a laundry routine and you won't have to think about it because it becomes a habit. After a few weeks, it will feel strange if you sit down to eat dinner before putting the laundry in the washing machine.

If you want to create a system for getting out of the house in the morning, set up a place near the door where you can put things that need to go with you. After dinner, set the table for breakfast and put out any food that doesn't need to be refrigerated. If you have a programmable coffee maker, fill and set it. Make lunch and put it in the refrigerator.

Put your briefcase, backpack or tote near the door and put in it anything you need to take with you in the morning, including library books, gym clothes or special equipment. Before you go to bed, select your clothes and accessories for the next day and hang them on the back of the bedroom door. Practice these rules each day and you won't feel rushed in the morning, which can completely change your outlook for the day.

You also can create boundaries around how many things you keep or how often you will do something. You can decide that you will file only when your "To Be Filed" stack reaches the top of its box. Until that time, you don't need to think about filing; however, once the box is full you need to schedule time to file. You might choose to go through your clothes twice a year and decide what you want to keep. You don't need to make decisions about discarding anything until the season changes and you adjust your wardrobe. You could keep magazines in a specific container and, when it's full, select the ones you can let go of.

Exercise 5 – Set limits

Choose an area of concern and create a system for dealing with it (mail, filing, laundry, groceries, etc.). Decide where, when and how you will do it, whether you need to ask for help from others and where things will go.

Room _____

Rules _____

_____

_____

Day/Time _____

People _____

_____

Containers _____

_____

After you complete the exercise, take out your calendar and schedule time to make it happen. Practice it regularly; remember that it takes time to create new habits. Before you decide that something isn't working, ask yourself if you really gave it the effort you needed to be successful. If not, try again.

If you follow the rules you created and the system still doesn't work for you, ask yourself where it broke down. Are you being realistic about how long it takes to do a particular task? Do you hate the room you set up for that purpose? Are you trying to cram more into your day without giving up anything? Are you attempting to do something when you're too tired? You need to be 100% committed to changing your approach in order to maintain the new behavior.

> The indispensable first step to getting the things you want out of life is this - decide what you want. — Ben Stein

Have you put off making a change because you think you don't have time? Instead of waiting until you can dedicate several hours to your goal, use small amounts of time to your benefit. When you have a few minutes between appointments, go through the paper on top of your desk instead of squeezing in one more phone call or email. While you're waiting for a delivery or a service technician, go through your reading pile and read or discard the things you've put there.

Thinking unrealistically about how long it will take to do a task can keep you from making progress. People tend to overestimate how long it takes to do things they dislike and underestimate the amount of time they spend on things they like. Set a timer to see how long you actually spend on specific tasks; you might be surprised by the results. In the *Habits* chapter we will discuss ways to make the most of your time.

The way to get the most out of your day is to do more when you have the greatest amount of energy. If you are at your best in the morning, use that time for activities that take a lot of effort. If you are more energetic in the evening, use those hours for tasks that require you to be alert.

I consider filing to be a low-energy task, so I don't do it during my high-energy periods; I usually do it in the evenings, when I'm too tired to be creative. If, however, filing requires your full attention to get it done correctly, then you'll need to do it when you're feeling sharp. Match the task to your strength; don't use your most productive time for checking email or your social-media status.

Finally, pick a place you enjoy working, whenever possible. If you have set up a home office in a corner of your basement and you really prefer working in the kitchen, the prospect of your paperwork getting filed is not good. Make your space attractive, accessible and functional and you are more likely to use it for the purpose you intended.

When you find yourself using a bedroom, kitchen, dining room or family room for an office or hobby room, find a way to make it work. Allow yourself to be comfortable in that room; create systems that allow you to quickly and easily put things away and you will be able to use the room for eating, sleeping or entertaining in addition to your projects.

Keep like items together, where you use them

During the **S**orting phase, you grouped together like items and you chose where to put them. Your system for keeping them in their new "homes" will depend on everyone putting them back. Make sure the spots you selected are accessible so you aren't picking up after everyone else.

Just like rooms, closets can be used for more than one purpose. A linen closet can hold light bulbs, batteries and healthcare products. A coat closet can hold sports equipment, backpacks and cleaning supplies. You can keep filing in the kitchen pantry. Look beyond what a closet is typically used for; think about where you use things and keep them nearby.

People tend to spend 30 minutes a day looking for things. If you habitually lose things, figure out where you are going to keep them when you are not using them. Be consistent about putting things back and you won't have to search when you need them.

Creating systems simply means knowing what you want to do and following through. People crave order, but it takes work. Start small, maybe with a place to keep your keys, and build on your success. Each accomplishment will make you feel better about coming up with additional systems, all of which contribute to making your life easier.

I have asked you to stick with your new systems to give yourself a fair shot at success; however, you also need to remain flexible. The process you choose needs to continue to work even when you've made changes in your life.

The rest of the book is designed to help you work on specific areas where you experience clutter. Use the techniques that have already been described, in addition to the exercises contained in each section, so that you achieve your goals.

When You Can't Let Go of Shopping

We live in a consumer culture. Marketing professionals convince you that you need what they're selling, partly by creating dissatisfaction with your life. That is why people often think that buying something new will make them feel better. Unfortunately, that feeling of pleasure can turn to remorse or even shame. People shop for reasons that often have nothing to do with need.

Exercise 6 – Clarify the cause

Why do you shop? Because you need something? As a reward for an accomplishment? To relieve boredom? Because you discovered a great deal? Think about something you purchased recently; write why you bought it and how it made you feel.

Item _____

Reason _____

_____

_____

Feeling _____

_____

_____

George Loewenstein, an economist, conducted research at Carnegie Mellon University that demonstrated how the anticipation of buying something you want creates pleasurable feelings. When you read about something new or see it on television, your anticipation of owning it can outweigh the pain of having to part with your money. It's hard to think rationally when you're excited about buying something new, especially when you think the item missing from your life is going to make it better.

You might share some of the same concerns about shopping that clients and workshop participants have expressed:

- I need to learn how to live within my means and know what I need, versus what I want.
- I want to stop buying things just because they are available and I like them.
- I use shopping as a quick, pleasurable "fix," then I forget about what I bought.
- I want to be able to relax and not use shopping as a comfort measure.
- I need to understand that if I don't "rescue" something, someone else will buy it.
- I think I would have more self-esteem if I could put money in the bank because I stopped buying frivolous items.
- I tend to shop when I'm bored at work and end up buying things I don't wear.
- I would like to buy only what I need to consume right now and not hoard or stockpile things that eventually end up going unused.

If you want to change your relationship with shopping, you need to develop rules about shopping behavior, just like rules you make for your stuff. Before you buy anything, question whether you already own something you can use for the same purpose.

Cooks make substitutions in recipes, stylists use existing accessories to dress rooms and mechanics make use of the tools they have on hand. Seriously consider the object you think you need before you buy it. If you're out of light bulbs, you can't sit in the dark; however, do you really need another pair of sneakers because they say they will improve your sports performance? Look at the things you have and see how you can create different combinations or use them for another occasion.

When you continually buy duplicates of things because you're not sure what you have, go back to your **ESP**. **S**ort the items and **P**lace them where you can find them, whether it's spices or scissors or socks. I have clients who tell me they have multiples of things because, when they see something in the store, they think "You can always use some [insert thing here]." Letting go of clutter means letting go of the need to buy on impulse.

If you are afraid of running out of something, keep a list on your refrigerator, in your planner or on your handheld device. You can have dedicated lists for the grocery store, hardware store, office-supply store, etc. When you are in the store, you'll know what you need and you'll avoid buying yet another paintbrush or box of paper clips.

When you bring in something new, let go of something you already have

Before you bring anything new into your space, identify where it will live. If you don't have room for something, you won't put it away and it will become clutter. When you are buying a replacement for something you already have, let go of the old one to make room for the new.

I encourage you to get in the habit of letting go of at least one existing thing for each new one you allow into your home or work area. That way, you don't accumulate more than you can use. When you buy new things and "save" them for some occasion, while continuing to use the ones you already have, you are wasting money and resources. You can keep clutter from building up and save money, too, by buying only what you need, when you need it.

A technique that works for many people is "The Pause." The next time you see something you think you must have, take some time to consider the consequences. Ask yourself specific, direct questions and be honest with your answers.

Exercise 7 – Pause

Ask these questions the next time you want to buy something:

Is it similar to something I already have? _____

Do I have room for it? _____

Do I have something else I could use? _____

_____

Could I buy it next week? _____

If I buy this now, what will I not be able to buy/do? _____

_____

Imagine the worst thing that could happen if you don't buy the item you want. For most people, there is no negative effect from **not** buying. If you answer the questions honestly and decide that you do need whatever it was you were considering buying, get it. If the answers make you realize you don't need it, you can avoid spending money on something that doesn't add value to your life. Putting some time between your initial impulse to buy and actually buying it can reduce your desire to acquire.

Now go back to the item you chose in *Exercise 6*. Do you still feel the same way about it? Have you used it? If you had used the techniques in *Exercise 7* before you bought it, would you choose differently?

There are no "correct" answers. The outcome of completing the exercises is to get you to think about what you could do differently next time. If you have to justify or rationalize your purchases, you probably don't need them.

To reduce impulse purchases, shop with a list. Whether you're shopping for groceries or furniture, you are best served by sticking to what is on your list. You can create a wish list of things you would like but can't afford to buy right now. When you stop spending money on things you don't need, you will be able to save up for the things you really want.

> *All problems become smaller if you don't dodge them, but confront them.*
>
> *- Adm. William F. Halsey*

In tough economic times, it's especially important to think about how you spend your money. Jeff Yeager, "the ultimate cheapskate," has written about going for a pre-determined period of time without buying anything. He suggests starting your "fiscal fast" by going for a week without spending any money. For one week, question whether you really need to make the purchases you want to make by practicing *Exercise 7*.

If you can get through one week of not spending, Michelle Singletary, author of *The Power to Prosper: 21 Days to Financial Freedom*, goes even further. Michelle asks readers to avoid spending money for 21 days on things that aren't absolutely necessary. The goal is to think differently about your relationship with money and the power that things have over you.

Shopping as Recreation

People who say that shopping is their hobby end up loading their homes with stuff they don't need. If you want to stop using shopping as a way to fill time or amuse yourself, you need to recognize when you do it and identify what you will do instead.

Dr. Lowenstein, of Carnegie Mellon, says that people who buy more than they need think they are "investing in happiness." Studies show, however, that once you buy something and are over the initial excitement, you no longer feel good about the purchase and start to look for something else to buy. You can learn to be fulfilled with activities that don't involve shopping.

Exercise 8 – Develop awareness

List some shopping guidelines. If you want to decrease the amount of time you spend shopping, set a limit. If you shop when you're bored or lonely, commit to avoiding stores during those times. If you want to save money for another use, envision that goal.

Occasion _____

Feeling _____

Substitute _____

Goal _____

Keep your guidelines on a sticky note and carry them in your wallet. Remind yourself that you don't need to shop to have fun. There are going to be people who are disappointed by your choice to let go of shopping as entertainment. Be prepared to defend your position without making excuses.

Bargain Hunting

Attention, bargain hunters! Research from Carnegie Mellon University, mentioned earlier, shows that the anticipation of buying something you want creates a pleasure response in the brain. Conversely, the research discovered that the thought of paying a high price for the item creates a pain response. When you see a great price on something you want, do you get excited about how much you can save?

The truth is you are **not saving** anything when you **spend money**; you are simply spending less. The greatest fiction may be the "buy one, get one free" sale. You are not really getting anything free. You are getting two things at half price. If you need two boxes of spaghetti and would buy them anyway, take advantage of the discount. But if you don't need two toothbrushes or pairs of shoes or jars of applesauce, you are spending money on something you might not use.

If you will use the second product in a reasonable amount of time, and you have a system for maintaining inventory, then you're doing well by getting it at half price. Otherwise, if it takes you a year to use up a box of cotton swabs, for instance, you're likely to forget that you have the second box by the time you need it. In that case, you may end up buying two more boxes when you see them on sale. Before you know it, you have accumulated more than you need and it becomes clutter.

A "good deal" is not a good deal if you don't need it, regardless of its price. You can afford to buy three shirts or pairs of shoes or pants, but is it a good use of your resources right now? Before you give in to temptation when you spot a sale, think about how often you use the item and how much space you have to store extras. Then decide if it really is a "bargain" for you to purchase in quantity. If not, save your money so you have it for something you really need.

I was at a household-goods store, replacing a broken salad spinner, when I heard two shoppers talking about a bargain one of them had just found. She was exclaiming about the price reduction, while her friend asked her what she would use it for. "I don't really need it, but it's a great price!" she answered.

Does that sound familiar? We often buy things that seem like great bargains, but when we get them home, they just create clutter. The next time you are in that situation, instead of thinking about what a bargain something is, ask yourself if you would still buy it if it cost twice as much. Would you buy it if it were full price? Do you really have a need for it, or are you just buying it because you can?

> **Live your today,
> not who you were or who you might be**

People often buy things that they believe are priced well, even though they don't need them, because they think they can use them in the future. Have you bought things for grandchildren that haven't been born yet? Have you purchased clothes that are too small because they were "a steal" and you'll lose weight to fit into them? Have you bought tools or materials for a hobby that you would like to pursue one of these days? How many of those items are unopened, unworn, unused and forgotten?

Don't buy for "someday." When you are tempted by "bargains" on things you don't need now, you are not using your money well. Just like you did in the Sorting exercise, when you thought about what to keep, take money out of the equation. If it only appeals to you because of the price, let it go.

During an economic downturn, more people watch what they buy. In fact, there is a popular movement of people who take pride in being frugal. Dan Ariely, a professor of behavioral economics at Duke University and the author of *Predictably Irrational*, expects shoppers to experience a "new, more thrifty pattern of consumer behavior." The result is that more people will shop for things on sale and spend more in discount stores.

Truly thrifty people shop for quality, not quantity. Instead of buying lots of inexpensive things you like, invest your money in one thing you love. Lee Eisenberg, author of *Shoptimism: Why the American Consumer Will Keep on Buying No Matter What*, suggests that if you are going to spend money you "Shop thoughtfully, choose carefully, think value."

Keep in mind that spending less is a great goal, but it's effective only if you're buying what you truly need. If you congratulate yourself for the deal you scored on something unnecessary, it's not a bargain at any price. Before you go shopping for anything, keep in mind what you already have and treat the pleasure centers of your brain to some other activity.

When You Can't Let Go of Clothing

Lots of people say they have too much clothing. It can be hard to accept that you have a limited amount of space to store your wardrobe. When you exceed that space, you need to make decisions about what to keep. If you are holding on to clothes you don't wear, it's time to let them go.

Some rationalizations people use for holding onto clothes they aren't wearing:
- It reminds you of a happy time
- You might have an occasion to wear it again
- You are keeping it as a spare in case the one you really like is ruined
- You used to wear it all the time
- You would wear it if you just had something to go with it

I have worked with several clients who completed large clothing purges. They can't comprehend how they had so much to begin with, and are amazed when they see the amount they have let go. Shopping mistakes, gaining or losing weight, or just changing taste all contribute to closet overflow if you put off making decisions about what you own.

What's most astounding is that there is always plenty of clothing left for them to wear after they choose the things they want to keep. I have not yet had a client who needed to restock after a clothing purge; rather, they found that they were able to access and enjoy the clothes that made them look good and feel good without having to search through things they weren't wearing at all.

Research shows that we wear 20% of our clothes 80% of the time. If you are hanging onto clothes that don't fit, don't look good or don't feel good, ask yourself if it's time to pass them on. Someone else can benefit from the things you aren't wearing and you gain the benefit of space.

Some of my clients are concerned about donating things to charity because they aren't "getting any money from it." When you donate to a qualified charity, you may be eligible to receive a tax deduction, which will benefit you. People often think they should be able to get cash back for things that they have bought and used. If you believe that your clothes are worth selling or consigning, and you have the time to pursue it, give it a try.

You may be successful selling clothes at yard sales or taking things to consignment shops, but you will not get back the amount you paid. People who shop at yard sales are looking for bargains; you will generally get what the item would sell for at a thrift shop. Consignment shops are looking for current styles, especially high-end brand names, and they will give you a portion of the sale after your item has sold. Don't be offended if they don't accept your clothes; they know what appeals to their customers.

In the earlier section on creating systems, we talked about setting up rules. If you have more clothing than you have room for, you need to set up rules for how many of each thing you will keep.

The only reason to keep is to enjoy

Starting the **ESP** process with a drawer, shelf or section of a closet, **E**mpty it and put everything on the bed. **S**ort and group like things. As you look at what you have, remove everything that is stained, torn or shapeless and put them in the trash. Put anything that you don't like, but that is still in good shape, into a bag or box to give away.

Looking at what you kept, pull out the things you really like to wear, and set them to one side. If there is anything else left, decide if you can let it go. How many of this item do you need? Can you be satisfied with the group of things you just chose to keep? Fold or hang the things you are keeping and Place them back in the cleared-out area.

> ### Letting Go, Real Life:
>
> During a workshop a woman asked me how many pairs of socks a person should have. I said that I couldn't give a definite number that would work for everyone; however she pressed me for an answer. She told me she does laundry once a week, so I suggested that 10 pairs of socks was probably sufficient.
>
> She answered that she couldn't possibly manage with just 10 pairs of socks because she walks in the morning and changes her socks when she comes home because they're sweaty, then she puts on a clean pair to sleep in.
>
> Given that information, she now needs at least 21 pairs of socks to get through a week. That number of socks might be unnecessary for many people, but it was right for her.
>
> When you consider how many of each item you are keeping, you need to look at your lifestyle, your schedule and your habits. What's adequate for you might not work for someone else. Decide how many things you need, based on what you will use and what you have room for.

This could be a time when you need to call for help. If you have trouble making decisions, ask a friend to help you separate the keepers from the things that need to go. You may feel nostalgic about an item of clothing that really doesn't suit you.

Even though you haven't worn something in a long time, the prospect of reuniting with it may bring up strong feelings. You may feel like you have invested time into the "relationship" with the object, which makes it difficult to let it go. Touching something also can complicate your ability to let go. In that case, you can benefit from having someone else hold up each piece of clothing for your approval.

If the stack of things you want to keep is bigger than the space you have, you need to think about letting go of some of them or finding an alternative storage space. Be honest: Is the item still in style? Does it fit? Does it look good on you? If not, consider passing it on to someone else who can enjoy it.

Set small goals for yourself, completing the same exercise until you have cleared every space that holds clothing, including storage areas where you keep out-of-season clothes. It may take longer than you expected, but working at it over a period of time will enable you to build on your successes.

You probably will find more clothes mixed in with other things or waiting to be cleaned. When they show up, don't automatically put them away. Look at them critically and make a conscious choice about keeping them or letting them go.

In addition to grouping like items together, you may benefit from creating categories, such as formal, work, casual or play. Separating clothes by function will help you find what you are looking for faster and allow you to get dressed without searching for things.

Some people like to group clothes by color and others like to create outfits that are ready to wear, right from the hanger. You can experiment with different systems if you don't already have one, but don't get caught up in finding the "perfect" way to arrange your wardrobe. The easier it is to put things away, the more likely you will be to follow through.

Whether you prefer to hang or fold clothes, configure your storage space to accommodate your preference. Typical closets are 22-24" deep, with one shelf and one hanging bar. If you have the basic closet setup and it isn't working for you, you can buy fairly inexpensive components that will give your closets more function. You can invest in a custom closet system, too. Either way, choose what's going back into the closet before you commit to a new closet arrangement.

When You Can't Let Go of Projects

I love projects. I love the planning, purchasing supplies, making lists, the image of what it will look like when it's finished. I don't, however, always love the actual doing. Does that sound familiar? If so, there are ways to work with your natural tendencies and keep clutter from building up.

You can fulfill your desire to be creative; however, you need to edit ideas and supplies, create adequate storage and schedule time for completing your projects. You also need to factor in time to put your materials away when you are finished for the day, but haven't completed the project. Clutter develops when you leave unfinished projects spread out in an area that needs to be used for something else.

> ### Letting Go, Real Life:
>
> I have accumulated crafting treasures ever since I was a child, learning new crafts and dropping others as the years passed. I finally realized that I will never have the time to do every craft that looks interesting, so I am concentrating on the few that I really enjoy: crocheting, card making and sewing. That meant paring back my supplies, including letting go of the ones I wasn't using.
>
> I never thought I could get rid of these "old friends," but I'm glad that someone else is having fun with them and getting some value from them.
>
> When you narrow your choices and concentrate on projects you really enjoy, you can stop buying and storing stuff you don't use.

Working on multiple projects can cause you to feel overwhelmed and exhausted, and can be expensive, too. Decide what you really, truly want to spend your time on and then stick with it to completion. For people who like the excitement of starting new things, this recommendation can be tough to follow.

Project clutter often occurs when you have trouble making decisions. You might be stuck deciding on a color, size or design detail. If you are unable to narrow down your choices, ask for guidance from someone you trust. Procrastination or perfectionism also could be keeping you from finishing projects. Refer to the *Habits* chapter to get ideas on how to overcome them.

> Much of the stress that people feel doesn't come from having too much to do. It comes from not finishing what they started. — David Allen

You might be unable to complete a project because you're waiting for someone else to complete a step. In that case, you need to plan your time to include delays. It might be tempting to start something else while you're waiting; however, consider whether you have time and space for both.

Break down complex projects into smaller steps so you don't struggle with the amount of work they require. Decide when you want to finish, when you are going to work on the project and how much time you will devote to each step. Like any other task you want to complete, put it on your calendar and plan to work on it regularly so you can accomplish it in a timely manner, with a minimum of stress.

When You Can't Let Go of Paper

The question most people ask me is what to do with the paper that ends up all over their homes and offices. Someone once predicted that computers would eliminate all of our paper; instead, it seems that we accumulate more than we ever did.

We continue to get newspapers, magazines, account statements, bills, flyers, newsletters, catalogs and advertisements. New purchases come with warranties and instruction manuals. Children bring home an abundance of paper from school. In order to remember things, we write notes on scraps of paper.

What are you supposed to do with all that paper?

People tend to hold onto paper because they are afraid of the consequences of letting go. If you didn't create the form, chart, report, booklet, statement or handout, chances are very good that you can find another copy somewhere. If the information is easily available on the Internet, you probably don't need to keep a paper copy.

When you can't decide whether to keep a piece of paper, ask the following questions:

- Will you refer to it?
- Do you have more than one copy?
- Is it something you're still interested in?
- Is the information relevant?
- Is it an original?
- Can you find the information somewhere else?

You might be holding onto papers that belonged to a project you completed, yet you aren't ready to let them go. If you are keeping the paper to remind yourself how hard you worked or how difficult the task was, you already know it; you don't need a stack of paper to confirm it. Ask yourself if the paper is adding any value to your life. If it's just taking up space, consider whether it's time to free that space for another purpose.

If you feel overwhelmed, you are not alone. You can break through the paralysis that keeps you from addressing the piles of accumulated paper. Like other projects, it's best to start small so you can avoid feeling overwhelmed and experience success.

> The ability to simplify means to eliminate the unnecessary so that the necessary may speak.   - Hans Hofmann

Begin by gathering the loose papers from all over the house. You can put them in a box, bin or laundry basket. Find something big enough to contain them for the initial **S**ort.

Take the first five pieces of paper from the top of the stack and set aside the rest. You are going to begin by working only on these five pieces of paper. Do not put something back in the pile if you don't like what you ended up with.

Your mission is to take action on each piece of paper, starting with the first one. What is the next, logical step for this piece of paper? You only have three choices: throw it out, file it or act on it (e.g., make a phone call, send an email or note, schedule it on your calendar).

Make an effort to maximize the amount of paper you trash or recycle; you probably don't need most of what you are keeping. You will come across things that aren't important to you anymore, even if you have held onto them for a long time. You also will be able to let go of things because the event passed or the offer expired.

File what you are keeping if you have a filing system already. If your existing file storage is overflowing or you're not sure how to set up files, you can assign temporary folders in a cardboard box. In the next section you will learn how to create a filing system that you can use with minimal effort.

You might not be able to take the next step on each piece of paper right away. The person you need to consult might not be available, for instance. If you can't make a business phone call because you're **S**orting at night or on the weekend, put a sticky note on the paper with the action you need to take and put it near the phone or in your bag to take to work. Commit to following through with it on the next business day.

If you were able to get through the first five pieces of paper quickly, continue the process with groups of five papers, and keep at it for 30 minutes. If you are struggling to make decisions about each piece of paper, you could benefit from calling in a friend or a professional organizer to guide you through the process. Either way, don't go beyond 30 minutes because you will likely feel bored or get distracted and then it will be harder to make decisions. You can set an alarm to remind you to stop. Choose a day to continue your work and put it in your calendar. Keep working in 30-minute sessions until you get through the pile.

There are some essential documents that you will keep because they are legally or financially significant. We will address those in the next section. If you come across any of these important documents in your initial **S**ort and you don't have a place for them yet, you can put them in a folder or clip them together and put a sticky note on top that says Vital Documents.

Creating a Paper Management System

Once you have dealt with your accumulated stacks, you can set up a system for incoming paperwork. It's important to do this because paper keeps landing in your home and work spaces.

You don't want to get to the point where you have to start all over again with a large backlog. The only way to keep paper from piling up is to address it regularly.

You will decide when, where and how you will handle your incoming paper. Don't put too much importance on **how** you will deal with paperwork, just start doing it, which takes the burden off you to do it perfectly. It's more important for you to try something than to do nothing and let it all pile up.

To stay on top of paperwork, you need to set aside regular time to work on it. On page 25 we talked about "hooking" a behavior to something you already do. You can handle paperwork during your child's homework time or while you watch a particular TV program. If you need quiet time so you can concentrate, connect it to something that's already part of your routine.

I advise everyone to schedule what I call "desk time," which is a specific time on the same day every week when you focus on paperwork. You don't actually have to do it at a desk; you can work at the kitchen table or on the floor. Wherever you choose to have desk time, though, needs to be accessible or you won't do it. You need to make it easy to get to your materials and the space so you can be successful.

You might schedule desk time three times a week if you have an enormous amount of paper to work with. If you use online banking and electronic billing, you might only do it once or twice a month. Whether you do it weekly or monthly, don't spend more than 30 minutes at each session. You are likely to get more done if you schedule shorter, more frequent sessions than if you try to plow through several hours' of paperwork at a time.

During desk time you will pay bills, balance your checkbook, reconcile statements, track insurance claims, make decisions about the paper that came into your home or office, file anything you will refer to and discard what you don't need.

You will process any paper that has come into your space since your last desk time and follow up on anything that is still outstanding.

In the days between sessions, you can do a daily quick **S**ort, get rid of obvious junk and put the rest in an action box or bin for desk time. Have one place where you can safely collect paper, where it won't get swept into a pile when the space is used for something else. Putting your pending paperwork in a bin, basket or box will keep it from getting scattered. It may take a while to develop the habit of putting all your paper in one place; however, the return for your investment is going to be less time spent searching and more time to do what you want.

Think about the entry points, where paper comes into your home or office. Once it comes in, where does it go? If it doesn't have a designated spot, it probably gets dumped and forgotten.

Exercise 9 – Entry points

List the types of paper that come into your space and how they enter (e.g., mail comes in through the side door, school papers come in from backpacks, research comes from the home office), then note the purpose, or reason you hold onto them.

Type of paper _____

Entry point _____

Purpose _____

Type of paper _____

Entry point _____

Purpose _____

Type of paper _____

Entry point _____

Purpose _____

Once you identify the entry points and purposes, you can decide where the paper needs to go. If a particular piece of paper has no purpose, like junk mail, it can get trashed or recycled immediately. If you get duplicate notices of events from children at the same school, get rid of those, too. You will get the most out of your desk time when you keep paper in only one or two specific spots, instead of having to choose from multiple locations.

You might have one file drawer for financial paperwork, one for memorabilia, one for career-related materials and one for medical information. If you have fewer papers, one file box or drawer might meet all your needs. The objective is to have only one place for each type of paper, so you know where to put things away and where to find them when you need them.

As you become more confident, you will be able to make decisions about your paper more quickly. Moving paper around wastes time, so handle each paper with intent. Although I don't believe it is possible to successfully touch every piece of paper only once, minimize paper shuffling by deciding what you are doing with each thing as you touch it. You might have to make a phone call, consult a family member or look up information before you can discard or file a particular piece of paper. If you aren't able to complete the action, put a note on the paper and schedule an appointment to get it done.

Shuffling paper is not taking action

Here is a typical scenario: You get an invitation to an event. You open it, read it and put it down. You find it a few days later when you scoop up paper from the counter. You set it aside, with the intention of checking your schedule. Now you have touched it two or three times and you still haven't made a decision about it. What will likely happen is that the event will pass and you will miss it, finding the invitation weeks or months later.

However, when you handle paper with intent, you open the invitation, make a note on your calendar to decide by a certain date and put the invitation in your tickler folder (see page 65 for information on setting up a tickler file). You don't need to touch the invitation repeatedly to make your decision and you don't need to think about it again until the date in your calendar, which allows you to respond in a timely manner

Your calendar can be used for more than just reminding you of birthdays, events and meetings. It can help you keep track of tasks, too. Write down when you need to pay bills, make phone calls, return books to the library and pick up dry cleaning. Make appointments with yourself to get things done, including desk time. Create deadlines for individual steps of a project. You will find more uses for your calendar in the earlier section *Creating Systems*.

> The discipline of writing something down is the first step toward making it happen.
> — Lee Iacocca

Using your calendar as a tool will keep you from writing notes on scraps of paper, then having to search for them or risk losing them. I recommend having one calendar and having it with you all the time. A large desk calendar, for example, isn't portable and wouldn't work well, unless you have a good system for transferring information to it.

Once you start using a wall calendar and carrying a pocket calendar and entering information into an electronic calendar, there is a greater chance that you will lose information.

Opportunities start to slip away when you forget to copy something from one calendar to another. Use your calendar consistently and you will be able to let go of multiple pieces of paper, along with the concern that you have to keep everything in sight.

Discarding unnecessary paper and creating a system for what you need to keep will help cut down on the amount of time you spend looking for things. Going forward, handle paper with intent as it comes into your hands. Start to do it regularly and it will become a habit.

Mail, Newspapers, Newsletters, Magazines, Catalogs

Most people say they get too much junk mail, yet according to the US Postal Service, 82% of consumers usually read some or all of the advertising mail they receive. In order to keep your mail from overwhelming you, you need to have a plan for it.

When you bring mail into your home or office, throw away or recycle junk mail immediately and put the rest of the mail in a bin or basket that you will address during desk time. Shred credit card offers so that they can't be used by someone else to open an account in your name.

Don't send unsolicited mail back to the sender, thinking it will reduce your junk mail intake. You can remove your name from distribution lists by visiting the Direct Marketing Association's Web site, www.dmachoice.org. You can opt out of credit card offers, catalogs, magazines and other mail offers. The DMA says signing up will reduce your unsolicited mail by up to 80%. I have done it myself and it works, for the most part, but a small amount of junk still slips through.

To stop credit card solicitations, go to the Consumer Credit Reporting Industry's Web site at www.optoutprescreen.com to remove your name from the major credit bureaus' mailing lists for preapproved credit card and insurance offers.

If you support charities with your money, have a plan. You can choose to send one donation each month to a different charity and schedule it on your calendar or send all your donations once a year. Either way, you will keep yourself from sending multiple donations from solicitations that repeatedly show up in your mailbox. Once you have decided who you will support, you won't feel bad about ignoring the others who ask for your money.

You can contact non-profits and ask them to stop sending you mail. You also can keep your name off charity mailing lists (and avoid getting calendars, address labels, greeting cards and other "gifts" that you don't need) by donating anonymously at www.networkforgood.org. They will send your donation to the organization you choose, without your name or contact information, so you won't end up on solicitation lists.

Most banks, telephone companies and utilities offer online-billing and payment options. You can also set up electronic payments from your bank if a biller doesn't offer the service. Along with reducing the amount of mail you receive, conserving paper and avoiding the cost of mailing checks, you can stop worrying about getting payments in on time. Electronic bill paying allows you to schedule automatic, recurring payments as well as sporadic bills.

Before you add your name to mailing lists for newsletters or event calendars, see if you can find the information you need on the Internet or in your local newspaper. Remember that each time you give out your address you are inviting someone to send you more paper.

Magazines and catalogs have a tendency to pile up in people's homes. Decide where you are going to keep magazines once they come in. Put them where you are likely to read them, whether that is in the bedroom, living room or bathroom.

Determine how long you are going to keep magazines, whether you have read them or not. I suggest getting rid of the previous issue when the current one comes in. If that doesn't work for you, choose whether you are going to keep issues for two or three months and stick to it. If you can't bear to throw away magazines, consider taking them to a school, hospital or doctor's office where someone else will be able to benefit from them.

If you get gifts of subscriptions to magazines that you don't want, suggest to the giver that you do something else to celebrate. When that isn't possible, some publishing companies allow you to transfer your subscription to another magazine that is in their collection.

If you get catalogs you don't want, you can call the companies who send them and ask to be removed from their mailing lists. They will probably ask for the number on the address label, so don't throw away the catalog until after you make the call.

If you enjoy looking at catalogs, create some rules around how long you will keep each one and where you will read them. Keep them all in one drawer, bin or basket so they don't take over your space and make it a habit to toss the previous issue when a new one arrives. If you want to order something, you can tear out the page of the item you like, along with the ordering phone number or Web site, and get rid of the rest of the catalog. Create a deadline for making a decision about purchases if you don't order immediately. Write the date on the paper and take care of it during your desk time.

Filing

Everyone needs a basic filing system. You don't need to spend a lot of money or develop an elaborate creation; the purpose is to allow you to find the papers that are important enough to keep. You might think about skipping this section because you have plenty of filing space, but consider whether you can find what you need when you need it. If you aren't using all your file cabinets but you don't want to let go of them because you might need them someday, think about what would change to make that happen. Whether you have lots of room for filing or just a little, you only need to keep what you are going to refer to.

For those of you who say you can't file because you need to see everything out or you'll forget what you have, I respectfully disagree. I will bet that you know where the coffee cups are in the kitchen, even though they're "filed" in a cabinet. You probably also know where your coats are hanging even though they're "filed" in the closet. You are confident that those things will be there when you look for them and you can develop the same confidence with your paperwork.

The only reason to file is to retrieve

If you dump papers because you "don't have time" to file them, you will waste an extraordinary amount of time trying to find what you need when you need it. Take a minute to put the papers where they belong and you'll actually save time in the long run.

When I refer to filing, I mean giving your paper a home, instead of tossing it aside. You might prefer to keep paperwork in three-ring binders instead of file folders. Some people use magazine files as their preferred collection method. Even established "pilers" can file; you can create piles for specific groups of paper and stack each of them in a labeled bin or box or on a labeled area of a shelf. As long as you know where to put them and where to find them, your papers don't have to be in a file cabinet. Work with your preferences so you can manage your paperwork successfully and quickly.

You can start out with a file box, crate or drawer. If you think you will be more motivated to use it if you have something attractive, buy a piece you admire; however, I recommend waiting to buy a file cabinet or piece of furniture until you see what you really intend to keep. Instead, you can start out with a plastic or cardboard box. Once you see what you have, you can shop for a more permanent solution.

Begin with one box of file folders. Some people respond well to color to help them distinguish categories. For example, you might use red folders for health-related files, green folders for finances and yellow for household. Buy one box of multi-color folders if it will encourage you to file; otherwise, stick to one color.

You don't have to use hanging folders, but if you do, buy 3½-inch tabs to replace the short ones that come with the folders so you don't have to abbreviate. Don't stagger the tabs; keeping them in a line will make it easier to move them around when you add or remove files.

Labeling your folders and containers allows you to quickly and easily find what you're looking for and put paper away when you're finished with it. The titles need to make sense to you, so think about what you would look for before you stick a label on something. You can write on stickers or print labels from a label maker or computer, but don't allow the process to keep you from moving forward with filing. If you can't decide what to call a file, write a label in pencil or on a sticky note. You can always change it later.

If you're concerned about having too much to file, consider what you're keeping. You want to hold onto paper that has an impact on your taxes or finances. You don't need to keep old receipts from the grocery store or restaurant meals unless they qualify as tax deductions. The same goes for checks to the dry cleaner or electric company.

I recommend keeping your tax-related information in a designated folder so you can access it when you're ready to file your return. You don't need to divide everything by month, but it is helpful to divide by category if you itemize. Just having it all in one place will allow you to avoid the frantic search when you prepare your taxes.

> Today's accomplishments were yesterday's impossibilities.
> - Robert H. Schuller

You probably save information that supports what you reported on your return in case you are audited. The recommendation is to keep your tax returns and any paperwork that reflects income or deductions (receipts, W-2s, 1099s, etc.) for seven years. Ask your lawyer, accountant or financial advisor if you have questions about what you actually need to keep.

You can keep bank accounts, investments, credit cards and other financial information in your income tax files if they have some impact on your taxes. Otherwise, you might put them in a *Finances* file, depending upon how much information you receive and what you choose to keep.

Another essential group of papers is your medical information, including test dates and results, inoculation dates, dates of medical procedures, injuries and illnesses, and a list of medications you currently take. You don't need to keep dozens of papers that say test results were negative or benign, but consider keeping the most recent report so you remember when you were tested. Create a file with the same information for each family member. It's a good idea to keep a file for pets, too.

In addition to keeping your medical information in a file, you can consolidate pertinent information into one document, which is convenient to take to new doctors' appointments and keep in your emergency-preparedness bag if you need to evacuate your home. The information also is helpful if you are taken to the hospital and you are unable to communicate.

If you have children in school, you might be keeping their report cards, psychological-testing results or progress reports. You can create files for each child's education records and move their school projects and memorabilia to a separate file.

You might have a collection of sentimental papers that you don't look at regularly, but that you want to keep. Gather them all together and mark the folder or box or drawer *Memorabilia* or *Mementos* or whatever label makes sense to you. Do not call it *Miscellaneous*, which really means nothing but a pile of stuff that you don't know what to do with. If it's meaningful enough to keep, treat it with importance. You can learn more about memorabilia and collections in the upcoming *Sentiment* chapter.

Keep your filing system simple so that it is easy to use. If you find that you have several files with only one piece of paper in each of them, consider combining similar files. It is better to have fewer files than more. You will save time and frustration when you can stop searching for what you need, so think in terms of broad categories and group similar items. Remember: The goal is to be able to put things away easily and retrieve them quickly.

Exercise 10 – File Index

Create a list of all the file categories you might use. After you label your files and put them away, you will have a reference so that you can find what you need quickly. I recommend keeping a copy on your computer and saving it as *File Index*, so you can update it whenever you add or change a file. Here are some file headings that might be useful for you, along with what can go in each:

Banking – Account information, current bank statement

Car – Repair records, insurance policy

Credit cards – Account information, current statement, current credit report

Decorating – Project ideas; information about completed projects; receipts for art, antiques, furniture

Education – School records for each family member

Employment – Resume, Social Security retirement record

Health Insurance – Plan information

Hobbies – Club information, contact lists

Home Improvement – Receipts for appliances, household repairs and improvements

Insurance – Life, Home, Long-term Care, Disability policies

Investments – Account information, current statement

Medical – Records for each family member, including test results, vaccination records, surgeries, medical procedures

Pets – Health records, licensing

Travel – Directions & maps, vacation ideas, frequent-flyer accounts

Warranties & Product Information – Documentation for items you own

Depending upon how much paper you choose to keep, you may be able to consolidate some of your files or you might need to create more files to contain everything. Before you file anything, ask yourself if you really need to keep it. Don't take the time to make files for papers you won't refer to.

Just like the categories you choose, the places you decide to keep your files will depend upon your needs. Think about where you would look for the papers and make it easy to put them away. Be flexible, you don't necessarily have to keep all of your filing in one place. You might keep some files in the kitchen because you refer to them more often, but financial files can go in your home office because you only look at them monthly. Do what works for you.

If you keep files in more than one place, list the locations on your *File Index*. Here is an example:

Location	File	Contents
File cabinet - top drawer	Finances	Auto Banking Credit Cards Insurance Investments Loans Retirement Warranties/Product Information
File cabinet - bottom drawer	Medical	Medical records Articles about healthcare
Binders above kitchen desk	Family	Education records Pets
Binders in family room	Recreation	Hobbies Sports Travel

Files need periodic maintenance or they become cluttered. When I ask clients if they have purged their files recently, the answer is often the same: "I don't have time." Make file maintenance a regular part of desk time and you won't have to schedule a block of time to purge files. When you put something away, skim the file and see if you can let go of something else. Using the one-in/one-out rule will result in your having less to sort through when you're looking for a particular piece of paper, which will save you time.

Some documents need to be kept in a more secure location. I suggest purchasing a water- and fire-resistant safe so you can store these papers at home rather than in a safe deposit box at the bank because you might need to access them when the bank isn't open. Buy a safe that looks like a file box, with rails for hanging folders, so you can label the files. Papers that establish identity or ownership and that are hard to recreate should go in the safe, including:

Adoption, custody and citizenship papers

Automobile titles

Birth certificates

Death certificates

Divorce decrees

Home inventory list, photos and receipts

Marriage certificates

Military records

Passports

Patents and copyrights

Real estate deeds, liens

Safe deposit box inventory

Settlement and divorce papers

Social Security cards

Stock and bond certificates

Trust papers

Will, living will, powers of attorney

While you're at it, make a copy of everything in your wallet and put it in the safe, too. Having your legal documentation in one place, protected from flooding and fire, will provide you with peace of mind. Just like your regular files, the files in your safe need to be updated periodically. Once a year is probably sufficient for most people. You can sort and purge files in the month of your birthday, at the beginning of the year, or when you are preparing paperwork for income taxes. Whatever you choose, make it an annual event that you record in your calendar.

Organizing Your Work Space

Whether you work from home or have a space where you schedule family activities or keep financial paperwork, almost everyone has a need for some type of home office. It doesn't require an entire suite of matching furniture; it can be as simple as a corner of a room.

Wherever you choose to locate your work space, make it convenient so that you actually will want to use it. I have seen many people customize a home office area that ends up unused because the owner doesn't like where it's located. The purpose of the office will help determine the location. You might want your workspace in a place where you can monitor your family's activities; however, if you are running a business from home, you probably want to be in a quiet area, away from distractions.

If you don't enjoy the space, you will avoid it and you'll end up with paper piles all over the house. When I wrote about "desk time" earlier in this section, I mentioned that it doesn't actually need to be done at a desk. Think creatively about your need for an office, as well. It doesn't need to be fancy; it just needs to be a place that allows you to work efficiently and effectively. You need a place where you can put the materials you use regularly and find them when you need them, without having to search.

> Never confuse movement with action. – Ernest Hemingway

You don't need much to create an office. To get started, all you need are adequate light, a comfortable chair and a desk or tabletop. If you will be working at night or in a room without windows, you might benefit from a desk lamp in addition to overhead lighting. I recommend spending money on a chair that you can adjust. Try out several before you make a decision.

If you are buying a desk, look for one that maximizes the amount of space you have so you can spread out your work. You also need have drawers for office supplies and filing. If you have a computer tower, look for a desk with a cabinet so you don't have to keep the computer on top of your desk or on the floor.

While you don't need all the latest high-tech gadgets in your office, it is helpful to have a telephone, printer/copier and paper shredder all in one place. Buying a printer that also is a scanner will allow you to eliminate more paper. If you have more than one workspace in your home, decide which will be the primary office and house your equipment there. You might consider buying wireless devices, which will allow you to use computers and printers anywhere in your home. A trash can and recycling bin at each workstation will help you get rid of unwanted paper immediately, so you don't have to remember to take it with you when you leave the room.

Homebuilders often include kitchen workstations in new homes. If your kitchen has a built-in desk, do you use the drawers for office supplies or are they catch-alls for whatever lands there? If you have several cluttered drawers, think about assigning a particular purpose to each of them: pet paraphernalia, arts and crafts supplies, grooming items, or whatever you use in that area. The kitchen may also be a convenient place to charge your phones and other electronic devices.

If the desk is used by multiple people, then everyone needs to know where things go and that they are expected to put things back when they're finished with them. You can buy all the great organizing products you like, but in the end, it's all about having a process that keeps the space from becoming cluttered.

I have noticed that people are fascinated by the contents of office-supply stores. I can't deny that there is something appealing about office supplies and you might be tempted to buy products you don't need because you think they'll improve your life. All you need, however, are some basic tools to get your work done; a few pens or markers, pencils, paper clips, a stapler and a pair of scissors should be enough. Your desk is not a supply closet; any surplus supplies can be stored in a cabinet or drawer in a marked container.

Some people like to be surrounded by quirky items while they work. If they won't distract you and might actually make the paperwork process more pleasant, treat yourself to fancy folders or whimsical paper clips or an unusual desk organizer.

Decorative pieces and sentimental objects can take up a lot of room on your desk. Find a place where you can put meaningful items so you can see them, but they aren't taking up room on your work surface. Don't make your desk a shrine to a person, hobby or your career. Your goal is to get your work done so you can leave your office and spend time doing other things you enjoy.

I prefer to keep the top of my desk clear, keeping most of my supplies inside a drawer. If you prefer to have things in sight, group tools, files and reading materials. Give each group a specific spot on the desktop and limit how many of each item you will keep out.

While I don't advocate the use of junk drawers, clients often ask where to keep miscellaneous objects that everyone seems to acquire. Look at what you have in your junk drawer. Is there a better place for some of its contents? Would you be better served keeping all your tools in a tool box in the garage or basement? Can you find a space in the linen closet or pantry for batteries and light bulbs? If these things end up in your desk, and you decide that is the best place for them, then put dividers in the drawers and group objects so that you can find them when you need them. I believe that your words lead to actions, so instead of calling it a junk drawer, refer to it as a "utility drawer." You won't throw junk into it and you won't allow it to get junky if it has a purpose.

While you're at it, look at the number of promotional items you have. The next time you attend a conference or go to a community event, think twice about accepting "gifts" of pens, calculators, letter openers, key chains, or magnets. I'll bet you already have plenty; you just need to find them and put them in an accessible place so you can use them.

Adam Pash, editor of www.lifehacker.com, says that the benefit of being well organized "is just the lack of anxiety that comes from a clean comfortable workspace where you feel like things aren't piling up and overwhelming you."

Keeping your workspace clear requires you to be aware of what you do. Piles of unknown paper on your desk are distracting and can keep you from accomplishing your objectives. When you finish using a file, put it away. If you need to do more research, have a holding place for active files, either on top of your desk or in a drawer. Store files that you aren't using, but need to keep in order to support your work, in a separate area and label it "Archives." You can dedicate a file drawer or an entire cabinet to archives, depending upon your work. Previous years' income taxes are archives, for example, as are inactive client files or records of completed projects.

> *Continuous effort, not strength or intelligence, is the key to unlocking our potential.*
> *– Winston Churchill*

I am a big proponent of "tickler" files, kept either on your desk or in a desk drawer. The tickler prompts you to take action on something that you put aside until a specific date. You can create your own tickler file by labeling 12 folders January through December and 31 folders 1 through 31 (one for each day of the month) or you can purchase a desk file sorter from an office supply store. Every month you move any papers from that month's folder into the appropriate day's folder.

You use the file to remind you what you have to do on a particular day. Directions, invitations, itineraries and tickets can all go in the file so you know where they are on the day you need them. I recommend starting your day by looking in your tickler folder for any work that has to be completed that day. You can keep ongoing projects in the file or you can drop in a piece of paper that directs you to follow up with paperwork or actions. You would put any work you don't finish today into the file for tomorrow or the next available day you have to work on it, allowing you to prioritize activities.

Keep in mind what you can accomplish realistically each day; don't assign yourself work when you're going to be in meetings all day or when you have to meet a deadline for another assignment. The purpose of the tickler file is to allow you to get things off your mind but keep your projects moving forward.

Most people feel that they have to get more done in less time. If you free your mind from details of what you need to get done in the future, you will have more room to achieve what you need to do today.

When You Can't Let Go of Technophobia

I meet a lot of people who are afraid to use their computers to assist them in letting go of clutter. Their fears often have to do with losing data, either from not knowing where information is or because of a mechanical failure. There are ways to prevent both of these from happening.

If you treat your electronic files like paper files, and name them accordingly, you will be able to find them. The challenge is that most people keep much more information in their computers than they do in filing cabinets and they aren't consistent when they name files. In addition, they often keep the same information in multiple files, without realizing it. Having more than one copy of an electronic document in different places becomes a greater problem when you want to update something and can't figure out which is the most current version.

You can prevent this breakdown from occurring. Instead of assuming that you don't have a document when you can't find it immediately, and downloading another copy, use a search function to see where an electronic document is. It's important to save documents with titles that you will remember, and group like documents together, so you don't have to waste time looking for them. You can even create a file index for your electronic documents, like you did for your paper files.

Just as it's easier to find things on your desk when the top of it is cleared off, it is easier to find things on your computer desktop when you don't have to sort through clutter. Making use of toolbars and taskbars enables you to keep a minimum of folders on your desktop. If you share a computer, have each person create an individual folder to keep information separate.

Because I don't like to see a lot of stuff on my electronic desktop, I don't leave work out. You, however, might want to keep active project folders on your electronic desktop when you are working on them, then put them back (like putting them in a file cabinet) when you're finished.

To prevent losing data to a power outage or computer malfunction, you need to back up your computer's hard drive regularly. You can use a USB flash drive, an external hard drive, or an online remote-backup company. No matter which method you choose, put a note on your calendar to back up your computer regularly. The method you choose to back up your data, and the frequency you do it, will depend upon how much storage you need and how critical the information is.

Using Technology

There are lots of ways to use technology that will simplify your life. One way is to minimize the amount of paper you keep. If you can access information on the Internet or as a document on your computer, you may be able to let go of a lot of the paper that builds up and keeps you from moving forward. You will need to keep some paper files; however, think about what you can retain digitally instead of storing so much paper.

The Internet makes it easy to access articles and recipes from newspapers and magazines. Instead of cutting them out, you can download them to an appropriate folder on your computer's hard drive. Having a printer that is also a scanner makes it convenient for you to save information to digital files, then you can let go of the clippings you've accumulated.

Because each document is marked with the date you created it, you will know how old any particular item is and you can delete it if you haven't looked at it. For example, you might have collected several articles about the same subject, some of which are several years old. If you haven't read them yet, consider letting go of the older ones and keeping only more recent information.

You can create "Delete by [date]" folders on your computer, too. If you haven't looked at a document by the date on the folder, you can delete it. This system may force you to actually look at the items you've downloaded so you can make decisions about them. Chances are, if you haven't needed them before the deletion date, you won't miss them at all.

You can ask people to send you information in an email instead of in hard copy, to reduce the amount of paper you have to manage. Most banks, insurance companies, utilities and brokerage houses will send you an email alerting you that statements or plan information are available on the company's Web site for you to review and download to your computer. In addition to preventing paper accumulation, you can access the records wherever you are, not just from home or work, when you elect not to receive information by conventional mail.

As I mentioned earlier, my favorite use of technology is to set up electronic payments from your bank account or credit card for recurring expenses. Automatic payments free you from remembering to pay any particular bill on time, eliminating late fees and protecting your credit score. Of course, you have to ensure there is enough money in the bank, just as you would if you were writing a check, but you don't have to worry about mail getting to the destination on time. Ask your bank or individual creditors if they offer this service.

Technology can improve your life when you have what you need, when you need it. Creating lists in word-processing documents or spreadsheets allows you to find information quickly. I recommend everyone create a list of medical treatments, with dates and doctors' contact information, which is invaluable in an emergency and helpful when you go to a new doctor. You could create a list of all the appliances in your home and when they were last serviced. You might find it useful to keep a list of books you want to read, movies you want to see or music you want to buy. Some people keep address lists for mailing holiday cards. The benefit of using any kind of electronic list is that it can be updated quickly and easily. You also can keep the information with you if you use a handheld device or smartphone.

Now that you're imagining all the possibilities for storing information digitally, be realistic about what you keep. Just because you have lots of storage space doesn't mean you should cram your computer files full. It's not about how much you can store, but about finding what you need.

Treat your computer just like your file cabinet and go through each folder periodically, deleting what you don't use or need. As you open folders, see if there are any old documents you can delete. While you're at it, clear your electronic address book of people you don't keep in touch with anymore.

As we discussed in *Creating Systems*, using a calendar allows you to keep track of the things and information in your life. Once you become comfortable using an electronic calendar, you will realize all the benefits it has to offer. Unlike a paper calendar, electronic calendars allow you to set alarms. You can use an alarm to remind you of an appointment or to let you know that it's time to stop an activity. You can also set recurring reminders for the first of the month, the third Thursday of each month or every Monday. Instead of having to write the information each time, you type it in once and set it for the frequency you choose.

I always suggest using the easiest and least expensive system for your calendar. If your computer or smartphone comes with a program or application, learn to use it. If it doesn't meet your needs, there are a lot of calendar and reminder programs, some of which are free; some have monthly or annual fees. I recommend starting simply and not spending time on researching all the different types of programs and applications available.

There are lots of electronic services that work in conjunction with your calendar. You can find Web sites that will send birthday cards for you, alert you when your car needs to be serviced, deliver products to your home or office on a regular basis, store your appliance manuals and allow you to track progress on your goals. Before you sign up for any service, make sure that it really is going to save you time and effort and, if there is a charge for using it, that the cost is worth the benefit it provides.

One free reminder service that is widely available comes from the public library. Check with your library to see if you can reserve books online and get email messages when books are due. You could, for example, choose one book each month from the list of books you want to read and borrow it from the library. You will make your way through the list and you won't have to store books that you aren't going to read again. If you have signed up for the library's electronic reminder system, you will get a few days' notice when your book is due, which could save you overdue charges.

You might be using technology already to watch movies or TV shows or to play video games. Creating a to-view list will allow you to rent or stream video to your computer or television and avoid having to store the media. There are a lot of ways for technology to help you avoid clutter. Start with one and you can add more as you become comfortable with the process.

When You Can't Let Go of Email

You might be experienced with technology and use it daily, yet you are afraid to let go of email messages. Or you might be able to delete emails quickly and regularly, but you can't stop checking for them. Once you develop a system for managing email, you will be able to view it and handle it with awareness, which will decrease the amount of time you spend on it.

Imagine someone coming into your home or office every day and handing you a big, fat stack of paper mail. Every day. You would have to attend to it regularly or you would become overwhelmed. The same thing actually happens, every day, with email. Because you don't have to touch it, it's easy to ignore; it's just sitting in your inbox, not bothering anybody. Just like paper that doesn't get managed, though, you will pass deadlines and miss opportunities when you let email become clutter.

A lot of people open email messages, take a quick look at the contents, then move on to the next one. Doing that is comparable to opening an envelope, looking at the letter and setting it aside. When you manage paper mail that way, you end up with a pile, some of which is important, most of which is junk, and you aren't able to find anything specific without a search. When you "nibble" at your email, you're essentially doing the same thing. You end up with an email box full of messages and you're hesitant to delete anything because there might be something important in there. People waste hours shuffling email instead of taking action on it.

Going forward, handle your email with intent, as if it were paper. There are only three actions you can take with email: delete, respond or file. Delete anything that doesn't interest you or impact your work. You can safely delete invitations to events that have occurred and anything that just says, "Thanks." To prevent confusion, delete emails containing outdated information and previous drafts of documents that have since been updated.

Process email like paper mail

To reduce the volume of email you receive, unsubscribe from lists that don't provide you with valuable information. Ask people to take you off their list when they forward things to their 100 closest friends. Don't respond to unknown addresses and don't give information to unsolicited emails.

Periodically I strive for the elusive "inbox zero," but as soon as I reach it, I get 10 new messages. Having an empty inbox, to me, is equivalent to touching each piece of paper once. It sounds like a great idea, but it isn't practical. Instead of trying to meet some defined number, handle each email with intent, and strive to move it out of your inbox.

Reply only to messages that require your response. If an email is sent for your information and you aren't asked for input, you don't need to thank the sender. Don't use "reply all" unless everyone needs to know the information; you don't need to clutter other people's inboxes and you don't want to increase the amount of return mail that it is likely to generate.

There are very few jobs that require you to respond to email instantly, although I have worked in offices where people call to ask if you got an email because you didn't respond immediately. If you work in that type of environment, you can set up an autoreply, instructing people that you will get back to them within a certain time frame. You actually might be better off not responding immediately, because the sender might have figured out the answer or added details in a follow-up note before you were able to reply to the original message.

Email is best used when you have quick information to deliver. You might use email to avoid having long conversations with certain people, but sometimes it's easier just to have a telephone or in-person conversation to discuss details instead of trading multiple email messages. You can keep the conversation focused by emailing a set of questions or suggestions ahead of time. If you're concerned about having a record of the conversation, you can sum up the discussion with a short email confirmation.

There may be times when you want a written record so you have proof of the exchange. If you work in an environment that requires you to verify your actions, filing email communications will become part of your routine. Don't print emails to hold onto "just in case;" conserve paper and avoid searching through files by creating folders in your email program and/or in your documents file to house them.

Some companies have limits on the number of email messages you can keep or how long you can keep them. Check with your IT department to see how long emails can stay in your "Sent" or "Trash" folders if you use those as holding spots. Periodically go through your archives and delete anything that no longer requires your attention.

Sometimes I leave messages in my inbox when I am waiting for a response or when I need to get back to someone. There are rarely more than four, so they don't build up and get lost. If, however, you hold onto multiple messages for pending actions, file them in folders that describe their contents. Don't have one big folder called "Pending email" that you throw everything in or you won't be able to find what you need. You can set up folders by client, project, department, due-by date, decide-by date, delete-by date, received date or any other label that makes sense to you. Before you start filing messages, though, consider whether you actually will refer to them. If not, don't keep them.

> We're at the point now where the challenge isn't how to communicate effectively with e-mail, it's ensuring that you spend your time on the e-mail that matters most.
>
> – Bill Gates

Set aside a regular time each day to work on email, instead of reacting to it every time the alert signals that you have a message. If you don't receive much email, you might check it once a day or once every few days. If your business involves a great deal of email contact, you can check your inbox two or three times a day. Some days your plan won't work because you have to attend a meeting or an emergency arises; however, stick to your schedule as much as possible to avoid having email build up. It is easier to find time for a few 10-minute sessions a day than to look for an entire hour each day to devote to email correspondence.

Exercise 11 — Managing email

Create your own rules for handling email. Be specific about the time of day and amount of time you will spend with each email account you have. Commit to specific actions for your inbox, sent mail, junk mail and trash, whether that means deleting, acting on or filing.

Email sessions will take place _____

_____

Each email session will last no more than _____ minutes

Email lists to unsubscribe from _____

_____

Emails that can be deleted immediately _____

_____

_____

Emails that don't require immediate action will _____

_____

Sent email box will _____

_____

Junk email box will _____

_____

Trash will be dumped _____

_____

When you allow email to interrupt you constantly, you aren't able to focus on projects. You do not have to stop what you're working on every time a new email message appears in your inbox. If the same people came to your office, instead of sending email, would you stop to talk to them or would you ask them to come back another time?

You close your office door when you're in a meeting or working on a task that needs your full attention. Compare closing your email program to closing your door so you can avoid interruptions. View email as a tool and don't allow it to keep you from moving your goals forward.

When You Can't Let Go of Sentiment

Items that create feelings of sentiment or nostalgia for the owner can be hard to let go. This is a challenge I see regularly with clients who attribute meaning to things that look meaningless to other people. What appears to be an ordinary old T-shirt might be a keepsake to someone.

People at my workshops always laugh when I ask them how many souvenir coffee mugs they own but don't use. Although you might have trouble letting go of them, it's important to remember that they're just things; you'll still remember the vacation or party or achievement without the mug.

When you let things take on qualities beyond their practical value, they take up more room in your life. They reflect how you see yourself, so letting go seems like losing part of your identity. Your accomplishments are real, however, and you don't need objects to validate them. Consider, for example, whether you need to keep every trophy that you were awarded for participating in events. Would it be more meaningful to keep just the first one or last one? Could you let go of all of them and only keep the one that you earned because you met a goal?

> **Let go of the object, keep the memory**

I meet lots of parents who have trouble letting go of their children's artwork, schoolwork or clothing. Instead of holding on to everything, I suggest keeping a few representative pieces to reminisce about. It's fun to see how a child's handwriting progresses; however, it isn't necessary to keep every school assignment. Keeping only the best examples of work will enable you to enjoy them, rather than being burdened by excess.

Holding on to clothing to pass down to a younger sibling is sensible; storing clothing that no one will use is not practical.

When you let go of outgrown clothing, toys or books, someone else can benefit from them. Display your appreciation by framing a special piece of artwork or clothing along with a photograph of the child. Limit the number of things you keep as reminders and enjoy them fully.

> ### Letting Go, Real Life:
>
> One of my clients had me clear out her linen closet while she was at work. I sorted the bed linens into three stacks: those that fit the beds in her house, those that were still usable but didn't fit any beds in the house and those that were torn, stained or worn out. When she returned, she went through the piles I had made and agreed on almost all counts.
>
> She pulled out two tattered sheets that not only were the wrong size, they were too worn to use, so I asked her why she wanted to keep them, given all the lovely things she had. She said that they belonged to her late parents and she felt that if she gave them up, she was giving up her parents.
>
> I asked her if she had other things that reminded her of good memories of her parents and she said she did. After she thought about it, she realized that it didn't honor her parents' memory to keep something that was of no use to her and only took up the limited storage space she had.
>
> Instead, we honored her parents by donating all the worn-out sheets and towels to the animal shelter, which she said would have pleased her mother.

People have trouble letting go when they believe that everything from their past, or from a loved one who has died, represents a strong memory and that they would lose the memory without the object. When someone has died, there may be an overwhelming desire to save everything that person had contact with. While you may feel like you are providing a tribute to your loved one's life, you are not showing respect for yourself or the deceased by taking on the entire contents of that life. It is extremely difficult to sort through years of accumulated objects and make decisions about each one. You might benefit from allowing an unbiased friend to guide you in decision making.

Maybe the hardest idea to accept is that objects are just things and do not represent a person. It is difficult for a lot of people to realize that letting go of something that a loved one owned does not mean they let go of that person. You can take pictures of things that don't fit your life but have special meaning to you; let go of the objects but hold onto the memories. Create a photo album or photo box to enjoy and let the things you don't need go to someone who can use them.

Exercise 12 – Reminiscing

Ask yourself the following questions to help you decide whether to keep a sentimental item:

Do you have multiples of the same kind of keepsake? _____

Do you have something else that reminds you of the event or person? _____

Are you keeping it only because it was a gift? _____

Does it make you feel good when you look at it? _____

Your reaction to letting go of it _____

_____

If you feel strongly about keeping a particular piece, find a place where you can display it or use it. You will know that you made a choice to keep it instead of simply surrendering to sentiment. If you find that it doesn't add value to your life, you will be able to let it go without resentment or guilt.

I inherited a set of silver-plated souvenir spoons when my aunt died. I didn't want them, but I held onto them for almost 15 years before I decided to give them away. I rarely thought of them because they weren't taking up much room and I didn't see them regularly. Occasionally I would think about doing something with them, but I never did. I finally faced the fact that I didn't like them and I wasn't getting any benefit from them. I'm sure my aunt would have been pleased with my decision to let them go instead of allowing them to continue to feel like clutter to me.

I encourage people to create a document, explaining why they have kept certain items, and keep it with their will and other important papers. Although I believe that you should not be bogged down by excess, I also believe that family members should know why certain things were meaningful to their owners. If you don't enjoy something you inherited, then you shouldn't keep it. If, however, you knew the history of an object, and you could use it, would you prefer to keep it instead of buying something else to fulfill the same purpose? When sentimental items are useful and desirable, they may be harder to let go. Choose carefully what you want to keep, considering your needs and your space limitations.

If you live with someone who is very sentimental, you need to respect the individual's feelings about mementos. Discarding someone else's treasured items can create problems that last for years. Ask the individual if he/she would be willing to complete *Exercise 12* and make some decisions about what to keep. If you need help, consider contacting a professional organizer to assist you.

Collections

Periodically someone will ask me how anything would ever become an antique if all the generations who came before us had thrown everything away. We need to realize that people had fewer possessions and made things endure far longer than we expect things to last today. Pieces were made in smaller quantities and often were used until they were unusable, so there are fewer of them to go around. Because people had few things and weren't replacing them regularly, they didn't have clutter, so they had less to discard and less to pass on to heirs.

Antiques become valuable because they have retained their usefulness and/or beauty and because there are few of them, not simply because they are old. In order to be a true antique, an object must be at least 100 years old. Things that are not that old often are referred to as "vintage," but that doesn't mean they're worth a lot of money.

Most modern mass-produced items will likely have little resale value, even when they are quite old. Keeping things because you have accumulated an entire series or you think they might appreciate in value are excuses for excess. The reason to keep things is because they bring you joy, not because they might pay off one day. In the meantime, you are paying with your time to maintain them and, if you have to rent storage, with real dollars to stash them away for "someday."

Your collection may indeed be marketable. You can take it to an appraiser for certification, then make sure that it is insured appropriately if you decide to keep it. For more unusual items, you can investigate what similar pieces have sold for on the Internet. If you're considering selling your collection, set a date to meet with a dealer or consignment shop or choose a date when you will list the items for sale on the Internet or in print. If you need to wash, photograph or otherwise prepare them for sale, put those tasks on your calendar, as well.

If you have so much stuff that it causes a problem for you, then it doesn't matter whether it's brand-new or antique. The difference between a collection and a mass of stuff is the way you care for it. Use the things you enjoy or display them so they can be appreciated. If you don't have enough room to show them all, rotate your collections and store the other pieces safely.

Garages, basements and attics are not usually good locations, due to fluctuations in temperature and humidity. Ideal places to preserve books, photos, textiles and paintings include closets and the space under the bed. For more ideas consult *Saving Stuff: How to Care for and Preserve Your Collectibles, Heirlooms, and Other Prized Possessions* by Louisa Jaggar and Don Williams. It is a very detailed book and is easy to read. You can go directly to the chapter you're interested in, whether your stuff is coins, stamps or your kids' macaroni art.

Letting Go, Real Life:

I was at the grocery store and I picked up a home decorating magazine while waiting to check out. The cover featured a breathtakingly beautiful room, whose walls were filled with floor-to-ceiling open bookcases. The shelving was painted a bright white and held a collection of blue and green vintage pottery.

The vases, bowls and other pieces were artfully arranged, with lots of room between them. I was struck instantly with the idea that I wanted to live in that room, surrounded by those beautiful objects. I could find similar ones at flea markets and thrift shops and I could display them on open shelving that I could build!

Then I snapped out of it.

What was I thinking? I don't want to live that way. I don't like to dust. I don't want to have things, even if they are beautiful, that I don't use on a regular basis. And I can't see myself spending time sitting in my living room, admiring the walls.

I have a few pieces of vintage pottery, but I use them; I don't think of them as a "collection." I used to have lots of collections, from teapots to baskets to quilts, but I let go of most of them, keeping one or two things from each group that I really enjoyed.

The problem with collecting is that you always need to have "just one more." Now I am satisfied with what I have. I don't miss any of the pieces I eliminated and I know that they are bringing pleasure to someone else, instead of taking up space in my house.

Did someone else start a collection for you? It begins innocently enough: You admire something and someone buys it for you. Someone else sees that you have that item and buys you another. Before you know it, you have a collection of seashell- or frog- or beer- or cat-themed items. You might not even like the things that now constitute a collection and yet you're surrounded by them. If you find it difficult to tell people you don't want these things, you will continue to amass them. It is far kinder to tell people you have stopped collecting and allow yourself to reclaim your space.

Don't maintain a collection you don't enjoy

Lots of people have trouble letting go of things that have been given to them. When you are given something that doesn't fit in your life, recognize the spirit in which the gift was given and then let it go. Life is too short to hold onto things that don't bring you joy. Take a look at the things you have been collecting; if they are simply taking up space without making you feel good about them, it may be time to let someone else enjoy them.

If you do enjoy your collection, elevate it to the level of art. Find a way to display it that pleases you. You could create memory boxes, scrapbooks, quilts or collages from the items. Just don't allow yourself to get so involved in imagining the possibilities that it keeps you from making choices and moving forward. Don't create clutter with a new project that you won't finish. Set a deadline and if you haven't completed it by then, either find someone who can do the job for you or decide that you will let the idea go.

When you are ready to narrow down your collection, determine how much you will keep and select the pieces you like best. If you feel strongly that the collection remain in your family, ask relatives if they are interested in the items you don't want. If you aren't able to give things to people you know, and there isn't a market to sell them, you can donate them and know that someone will make good use of them.

When You Can't Let Go of Habits

People regularly tell me that they can't change because they are creatures of habit. My answer is that you are more likely to be successful because you've already shown that you can maintain a routine.

Did you have a great system for filing your paperwork once, but instead of filing, you've been piling lately? Did you put things away until you had kids and then you started to settle for dumping in any available container so your house looked tidy? Did you stop doing household chores regularly because you were so tired from working long hours? Did that lead to buying things you already had because you were too tired to look for them?

You can let go of old, unproductive habits and create and maintain new ones. You can return to positive habits you once had, too. You've probably heard the saying "It's just like riding a bike." People usually say it when they mean that you can pick something up that you haven't done in a long time. It could refer to any number of actions that you stopped doing. Whether it's something you truly enjoy or just something that needs to get done to make your life easier, you can get "back on the bike."

> *Courage is saying, "Maybe what I'm doing isn't working. Maybe I should try something else."*
> *— Anna Lappe*

Take a look at where you are now. If you want to make some changes in your life, you need to do something different. When you set guidelines for yourself, you are more likely to be successful. Whether you want to eat better, train for a marathon or clear clutter from your life, you need a plan or you won't establish new habits.

Go back to page 18 and set a goal to let go of an old habit or start a new one. Decide when you are going to start, how much time you are going to work on it, how you will know when you are on target and whether you have the tools and ability you need to be successful. Create a contract with yourself and, if you have trouble following through, ask someone you trust to help keep you accountable.

Exercise 13 – Kick the habit

Choose one habit that you would like to let go of. If you have more than one, work on one at a time. You need time to establish a new habit before you add yet another behavior change. "Stop having clutter" is not a habit, but leaving clothes on the floor is. So is buying things you don't need. And keeping things that aren't useful. Be specific about naming the negative behavior. What causes it? What can you do differently? Could you move furniture or change where you keep something? Create a reward for yourself when you have met your goal.

I used to (old habit) _____

_____

Now I (substitute new habit) _____

_____

Cause _____

_____

Space modifications _____

_____

Reward _____

Remember that it takes at least 21 days of practicing a new behavior before it starts to feel like a regular part of your life. Some days it's hard to have a positive attitude. Maybe you're not feeling well or you're trying to fit too much into your day, or things just don't seem to be going your way. Everyone is entitled to an off day, but if you allow yourself to get dragged down by negativity, you are more likely to fall back on unproductive habits.

> ### Letting Go, Real Life:
>
> I worked with a client who was experiencing significant clutter in her small apartment. We started out with her entryway, which opened directly into the living and dining rooms. Before our first visit she said that she dreaded going home, which was functioning only as a storage unit and a place to shower and sleep. There was nothing appealing about it at all, despite the lovely furniture and beautiful accessories she had, but couldn't see.
>
> After one three-hour session, where she let go of paper, trash and some things she no longer wanted, we put what she was keeping in appropriate places and rearranged the furniture to make the space more useful. She was delighted that she could see the difference in her home in such a short time.
>
> She actually walked outside and came in the front door, just to see what it felt like, saying, "Aaah, home." She said that she could invite people over and feel good about it. Once the surface clutter was removed, we came up with a list of "rules" to keep her from returning to her old behavior. With the guidelines spelled out for her, she believed that her attempts to create new habits would be successful.

If you really want to make a change, you can find a way to accomplish it. It probably will not be easy, but it definitely is worth it. Wendy Wood, a professor at USC, says that to change behavior, "you must change your environment, not just try harder in the same old situation." In other words, willpower alone will not make things different. When you restructure your space, you will be more likely to succeed.

You can reframe a negative situation by looking at it in a different way, which can turn around your thinking. You can reframe the way you refer to your habits, too. Rather than saying "I will never be able to get all this done," change your thoughts to "This is a big job, but I can accomplish it by breaking it down into steps and working at it over a period of time." Instead of believing that you can't do something, believe that you can. Be realistic and think positively about the outcome to make it happen.

Value Your Time

Every day people tell me they don't have enough time to create and maintain new habits. You might believe you don't have the time to exercise or put things away or finish projects. I respectfully disagree; you have the same 24 hours each day that everyone else gets. How you use it is up to you.

Here is what people in my workshops have said about time:
- I have no real sense of time and the passage of it.
- I have plenty of time, I just don't know how to use it properly.
- Our lives are crazy and I feel like I have no time for anything.
- If I were living consciously and deliberately, my life would be less chaotic.
- I want to simplify my life and stop wasting time.
- I have to find more time to enjoy my family, our home and our life instead of trying to catch up all the time.

Each of these people believed that there weren't enough hours in the day to accomplish everything they needed to do. Once they paid attention to how they were spending their time, they realized that their habits led them to be unproductive. I am not going to suggest that you rigidly structure your day so you can account for every minute; instead, I encourage you to look at what you are doing and let go of habits that keep you from being successful. Only then will you be able to focus on what is meaningful.

Some part of your day is used for sleeping, eating and conducting personal hygiene. If you have a job, you spend time working and probably commuting, too. If you have children, you need to care for their needs. When you don't schedule things that you want to do, in addition to the things you have to do, you allow yourself to feel like a victim of time. The reality is that you choose how you spend it. According to a 2007 article in *Time* magazine, Americans spend more hours watching TV than any other activity besides working and sleeping.

In time-use studies, participants are asked to write down everything they do and grade the tasks in order of importance. If you believe that tracking your time will help you be more realistic, then keep a record for a week and figure out what you can change so you can achieve your goals. You don't have to keep a detailed log, however, to change your habits.

Early in my management career I went through time-management training; the theory was that you could get more done if you could just manage your time. The truth is that you cannot manage time; all you can do is manage yourself in the time you have.

Awareness of time contributes to conscious action

There are going to be occasions when it takes longer than you predicted to finish a project. There will be other instances when someone gets sick, transportation is unreliable or you forget about a meeting. You might choose to work on other activities to avoid a task you don't enjoy. When you neglect something, take responsibility for accepting that things didn't work out as planned, instead of relying on the habit of saying you didn't have time.

Going forward, think about reframing the way you refer to time. Instead of saying that you didn't have time for an obligation, admit that you chose to do something else instead. Saying, "I haven't made the effort to do that yet" makes it a conscious decision on your part.

Here's an example:

You are in the habit of saying: *I didn't have time to file paper.*
Substitute: *I chose to* [whatever you did] *instead of filing.*
or
I decided that filing isn't as important to me as I thought.

You can change your habits and accomplish more each day. The objective is not to pack as much as you can into each hour, but to achieve your goals in the time you have.

Commitments

When you value your time, you realize that you can't do everything and that sometimes your choices might disappoint other people. You may find that it's hard to let go of the habit of saying "yes" to others when you really want to say "no." Learning that skill will go a long way to reducing stress and increasing productivity.

> *"No" is a complete sentence.*
> *— Annie Lamott*

Some people continue to agree to do things, even though they are overburdened, because they want others to think highly of them. When you allow yourself to become the key player for every committee, volunteer project and extracurricular activity, you are taking time away from what you need to accomplish. Trying to squeeze one more thing into your schedule will probably result in someone or something not getting the attention required.

If you want to make the most of your time, you need to let people know you are serious about protecting it. I teach clients to use what I call "the authentic no" when they don't want to add another commitment to their schedules. Instead of saying that you're not sure or you'll have to think about it, just say "no." You can come up with a reason, so you don't feel like you're being rude, but you don't have to make it elaborate and you don't have to make excuses. The next time someone suggests you participate in an activity that isn't a priority for you, try using one of these responses:

> *I'm not able to take on another project at this time.*
>
> *I wouldn't be able to give it the time it deserves, but I can recommend someone else who might be able to help.*
>
> *I can't chair the program, but I can work for two hours at the event.*

Author and professional negotiator William Ury says, "In order to say yes to what's truly important, you first need to say no to other things."

How do you want to spend your time? You need to decide what is most important to you. Don't allow other people to pressure you into doing things that take time away from your priorities.

Productivity

In the first section of the book, *Creating Systems*, we talked about a collection system. Consistently using your notebook, planner or calendar will allow you to let go of anxiety about how you use your time. You put appointments on your calendar and set aside enough time to get to them. If you are chronically late, it's because you take on too many activities or you don't allow enough time for each of them.

I recommend starting and ending your day with your calendar. At the end of each day, appreciate what you have accomplished and reschedule anything that you didn't complete. Be realistic about what you schedule for yourself. Don't pack your day too tightly; set aside time for travel, meals and occasional interruptions. Plan for things you enjoy, too, so you remember to do them.

At the beginning of each day, look at your calendar and see if there is anything you can let go of. Are you doing something that no longer has a benefit? Can you delegate a task or exchange with a family member or colleague? Things that you dislike may appeal to someone else, who could get them done with less effort. Just because you always do something doesn't mean you have to continue to do it.

> *Time is what we want most, but what we use worst.*
> *– William Penn*

Given everything you want to accomplish, ask yourself what absolutely must be done that day. I encourage clients to create a Two-Do list so they achieve what is important. No, that's not a typo, but a request that you remain realistic about your priorities. At the beginning of each day, make a list of two high-priority tasks you need to do that day. Schedule time to work on your Top Two each day and give them your full attention. Whenever possible, start them early in the day, so you can make progress before you get interrupted. The only way you will move forward is by recognizing the importance of your goals.

If you are afraid that you won't remember to check your calendar, "hook" it to a habit you already have. For example, if you start your day with a cup of coffee or tea, associate checking your planner with getting your drink. If you check your email before you do anything else, make your next task checking your schedule.

The reason to check your calendar regularly is to allow you the freedom to make choices based on what you want to accomplish. Instead of rushing to get things done, you have the ability to plan and act deliberately. Once you develop the habit of checking your calendar before you take on a commitment, you will become more aware of how you spend your time.

Exercise 14 – Maintaining focus

Periodically ask yourself if what you are doing is the best use of your time at that moment. By focusing on your priorities, you can avoid having one of those "I was busy but I didn't get anything done" days.

Is this the best use of my time right now? _____

Does this action support my goals? _____

If not, why am I doing this? _____

_____

How can I get back on track? _____

_____

Consider what you want to accomplish and how much time you have to spend on it. If you find yourself veering off task, create a system for getting back to work. You can use a timer to build in breaks, determine rewards for finishing a task or ask someone else to remind you of deadlines. Think about what will work best to encourage you to be productive and avoid wasting time.

Attention/Distraction

With all of the electronic devices people use, in addition to books, newspapers, magazines, movies, advertisements, etc., it's no surprise that adults feel their attention is constantly diverted by something new. If you are easily distracted, you know that it takes you longer to work on projects and that you have trouble finishing what you start.

There is always going to be something more interesting to do; the challenge is to make progress on your priorities. While the saying "Out of sight; out of mind" has a lot of truth in it, I never hear anyone say, "In sight; in mind." When items are in your field of vision, they can distract you and keep you from accomplishing your goals. If you know that you are distracted easily when there is too much to look at, you need to keep your space uncluttered. Otherwise, you flit between tasks, which is inefficient in terms of both time and energy. If you are distracted by sounds, you need to turn off the television or radio, the signal on your email program and the ringer on your phone so you can concentrate.

> Man has turned his back on silence. Day after day he invents machines and devices that increase noise and distract humanity from the essence of life, contemplation, meditation. —Jean Arp

Interruptions can overwhelm you when you work in an office. Studies show that the average manager is interrupted every 8 minutes and that it takes 20 minutes to get back to the level of concentration experienced before the interruption. You need to protect your time or you will be acting on other people's priorities instead of your own. Even if your job is focused on attending to other people's needs, you need to be able to complete assignments.

Julie Morgenstern, organizing and business productivity consultant, classifies interruptions into three types, which I have condensed to: Critical, Important and Insignificant. Critical interruptions have an impact on someone's health or a company's viability. Important interruptions involve answering questions for a client, coworker or subordinate. Insignificant interruptions occur when someone else has time to waste and uses you as an outlet.

Minimizing insignificant and important interruptions will lead to greater productivity. Make it easy for people to answer their own questions and help themselves to information. FAQ (frequently asked questions) sections on Web sites and self-service areas to pick up forms in offices are two examples of allowing users to get the information they need without interrupting someone. Think about the reasons people interrupt you and see if you can set up systems to minimize them.

When you need to devote your attention to a project, let people know that you are not available to them. If you don't have a door to close, you can put a note on your entryway that says you are working on a project, and request not to be interrupted for a specific period of time. Minimize distractions by turning off your phone and closing your email program.

If you are interrupted constantly by your cell phone, be cautious about giving out that number if it is not your primary means of contact. When you make yourself available at all hours, people will expect you to resolve their concerns immediately.

When someone asks you if you have a minute, and you don't, say so. Ask if you can get back to him or her and suggest a time. People will appreciate knowing they can count on your complete attention later on rather than feeling rushed or having you half-listen while you do something else.

While you're working on a task, you might remember something else you need to do. Instead of stopping what you're doing so you can attend to something else, write a note to yourself, send yourself an email or call yourself and leave a voicemail message. Don't allow the distraction to get you off track; schedule it for another time, keeping in mind what you really have to do right now.

There are going to be times when you have to stop while you're in the middle of something. You might be making great progress but you have to leave for a meeting, or there is an emergency that needs your immediate attention. When you're interrupted, you want to be able to return to where you stopped reading or continue writing the report you started.

Leave a reminder when you're interrupted

Julie Morgenstern suggests writing a "Next Action" note, which "can eliminate reorientation time," and enable you to get back to work quickly. You can stick a note on a folder, on your computer monitor or on the page you were reviewing. Note the place you stopped and what you need to do to get back to work.

Multitasking

You might be proud of the fact that you can accomplish several things at the same time. While multi-tasking can be useful in some situations, it can cause you to lose your focus. You can combine low-level tasks that don't demand concentration, like folding laundry while you're watching TV or sorting business cards when you're on hold. When you're involved in an important project, though, working on another obligation at the same time is probably not a good idea. Some jobs require your undivided attention in order for you to be successful.

What causes you to do multiple things at the same time? Is it because you have lost focus or because you think you can get more accomplished by doing several things at once? In actuality not only do you **not** achieve more, you are more prone to errors. If you lose focus, ask yourself if you are bored. If so, take a break or work on something else. If your mind wanders and you think about other things you need to do, write them down.

> ### Doing two things at once is not productive when you have to refocus

When you try to work on two things at the same time, you actually are not sharing your attention between the two; instead, you are switching focus, which constantly redirects your attention. This leads you to forget what you were doing. Since you're only giving part of your attention to each task, you're not doing either one of them very well.

Your brain can't process multiple activities at the same time. Linda Stone, speaker and writer, created the term "continuous partial attention" to describe what people do when they try to talk on the phone, type a report and check email at the same time. You are not fully present for any of those actions. It takes your brain approximately 10 seconds to shift between competing tasks and when your attention is diverted you're more likely to make a mistake. In addition, it probably takes more time than if you had done each task successively.

Years ago, when multitasking first became a business trend, I gave in to it. I thought that the more things I did, in the least amount of time possible, the more productive I would be. Then I realized it didn't work. Now I counsel people to do fewer things and finish them before starting new things. Instead of rushing and feeling stressed, slow down and concentrate. Choose what is most important to focus on and get it done.

Procrastination

A standard definition of procrastination is "avoiding an action or task by focusing on some other action or task." You procrastinate when you don't do something that needs to be done, even though it would make your life easier, save you money or further your personal or professional goals.

If you are putting off doing something, think about how much it means to you. If it doesn't add value to your life, consider not doing it at all. If, however, it's something you need to do for your work, your health, your family or your happiness, start by starting. Take a small step toward completion and continue to take small steps, keeping the project at the top of your priority list until you finish.

> Many of life's failures are people who did not realize how close they were to success when they gave up.
> – Thomas Edison

You might feel stuck or ashamed because you let people down when you don't follow through. Just because you procrastinate about doing something doesn't mean you are lazy. Maybe you avoid doing something because you think you aren't capable. You might not do it because you don't have the right tools. You could put something off because you have too many other things to do. Each of these reasons is valid for you. The objective is to figure out what is holding you back so you can get the job done.

People often procrastinate because they think a task will take too long. What I find is that they spend more time dreading a task than doing it. The energy you expend putting it off is usually greater than the energy it would take to complete it. In addition, starting projects and not completing them may increase your stress level, along with creating physical clutter.

The anticipation is always worse than the reality

If you believe that a task is going to take a long time, you might set it aside until you "find the time." Unfortunately, many projects fade away because that "found time" never materializes. There is no later; you only have now. If you really want to do something, you need to put it in your schedule and make it happen. This is true of projects, errands, even self-care.

When you find yourself making excuses about why you haven't completed something, you are procrastinating. You might use one of these reasons:

- It's boring. If so, commit to doing a little bit, either selecting a period of time or a piece of the project. I have found that a lot of my clients get excited when starting something new, but lose interest before they finish.

- You haven't established a goal. In that case, review *Goal Setting*, starting on page 18. Plan to spend time working on tasks that are important to you. Putting off a deadline will only prolong the agony, not encourage you to finish.

- You're afraid you're not going to do the task perfectly. Read *Perfection*, starting on page 103. Commit to taking some action or choose not to do it at all.

- You don't feel competent about making decisions. The section on *Decision Making*, starting on page 104, will help you. Procrastinators often lack confidence in their judgment.

- You never seem to have enough information. Read *Data Gathering*, starting on page 106. You can work on changing your habits to counteract "information-fatigue syndrome."

- You enjoy the thrill of doing something at the last minute. Look at *Crisis Mode*, starting on page 108. You can set boundaries when you are addicted to excitement and chaos, allowing you to accomplish what you need to do.

Letting Go, Real Life:

When I had the carpet replaced in my house, the installers broke the legs off my jewelry armoire and I wasn't able to get the company to repair or replace it. For three years, I looked at that poor, forlorn piece of furniture, standing upside down in my bedroom. I could still use the drawers, but I wasn't able to open the side doors. Although it was functional, every time I looked at it, which was just about every day, it reminded me of a negative experience.

I had the tools to fix it, but I wasn't sure I had the expertise and I was sure it would take a long time to figure out. One day I finally decided that I would take a shot at fixing it. There was a piece of wood missing, which made it a challenge to engineer a solution, but I tried what I thought would work.

The result? I was finally able to stand the jewelry armoire back on its legs and hang my necklaces on the doors, allowing me to see everything I had. The whole process took less than 15 minutes. I was so proud of myself, I told everyone I knew what I'd done. Why had it taken so long to do such a small task?

Sometimes we let the feelings about completing a task take over the reality of just doing it. Taking a few minutes each week to address these nagging issues keeps them from growing into overwhelming problems.

People who are living in chaos often think they'll never be able to dig themselves out. I have one piece of advice for anyone who has too much going on: Finish what you start. It may seem simple, but if you are someone who leaves tasks half-finished all over the house or workplace, this idea is life changing.

Examples of taking tasks to their logical conclusions include:

- Throwing away the empty package when you finish using something
- Putting the dirty dishes in the dishwasher or sink
- Sorting the mail when you bring it in
- Putting things back when you finish using them

Most of these tasks can be completed quickly. Remember David Allen's "two-minute rule." If an action can be completed in less than two minutes, just do it and move on. You can sort mail, write a check, change a light bulb or read a short article in two minutes or less. Completing quick jobs gives you a sense of accomplishment and keeps clutter from building up. Using short bursts of time also allows you to complete tasks that would grow and require long stretches if you put them off.

In his book, *Getting Things Done*, David Allen suggests you ask yourself "What's the next action?" when you work toward achieving your goal. When you decide what needs to be done next, you can prepare materials and schedule time to do it so you can be successful. Knowing what to expect can reduce the amount of time you spend thinking, worrying and putting things off.

Think of each task as having a beginning and an ending. Decide how much time you can commit to working on it and schedule an appointment for yourself to complete just that much. When the time is up, decide what the next step will be, schedule it and put the work away. Write down where you ended so you can get started on the next phase without having to remember where to pick up. Schedule the next step and continue the pattern.

Exercise 15 – Finish What You Start

Challenge yourself to consciously end each task you start. You may not be able to complete an entire project, but you can take it to a logical stopping point instead of leaving it hanging around. Create a plan for an activity that you're involved in now so you can see it through to completion. You may have to repeat the exercise several times before you finish.

Project _____

Stopping point _____

Next Action _____

_____

Accept that there are jobs that you don't really enjoy. By breaking larger, complex projects into small, manageable tasks you will be able to see progress. Set up rewards for completing small steps toward achieving your goal if that gives you the incentive to continue.

I use the term "productive procrastination" to describe what happens when you put off an important task to work on another one that is equally important. Delaying work because it doesn't involve a big payout when you have other, high-priority work is not procrastination. Having made that distinction, however, I find that more people have issues with procrastination than with having too much work.

Sometimes you make a decision by not taking any action at all. By not making a decision you've shown that the task isn't that important. If you fail to complete a project or follow up on an activity, maybe you need to stop procrastinating and just let it go.

Perfection

People often are surprised to learn that some perfectionists procrastinate. If you think you can't do it perfectly, what's the point of starting, right? The reality, though, is that you spend so much time worrying about the outcome that you could have completed the task in less time and with less anxiety.

If you wait for the "perfect" time or circumstances or system before you commit to action, you are making a choice by not choosing and allowing the details of your life to overwhelm you. Don't allow the idea of "someday" keep you from accomplishing what you need to do today. Some future event that you dread or anticipate might not even happen.

It bears repeating that a system is just one part of the whole process; your habits play a large part in your success. Constantly changing systems because you haven't found the perfect one yet is a guarantee that you will not succeed. Learning to live with "good enough" can be difficult, but it's a skill you can develop. Give yourself time to try a new way of doing things before you declare it (or yourself) a failure.

Perfectionists often say "I should" when questioned about how they manage tasks. I hear those words several times a week from clients:

> *I should return that scarf.*
>
> *I should give that box to my brother.*
>
> *I should send birthday cards to everyone in my family.*
>
> *I should put my clothes away.*
>
> *I should exercise every day.*
>
> *I should pay my bills online.*

They are surprised when I ask them why. Why "should" you do something? Because someone told you to? Because it will improve your life? Because everyone else does it? Rephrase the

103

statement and see if it still seems true. Instead of saying "I should," say "I want to" or "I plan to." When you feel obligated to do something, but there is no incentive for you to do it, you procrastinate. If you can reframe the behavior to make it meaningful, you are more likely to do it.

If you don't want to do the task you've been putting off, then don't do it. You will have to consider the financial, legal and health implications of your decisions; you are an adult and you have to live with the choices you make. Most of the things you choose to let go, however, probably will not result in major crises. Instead, you will have more time to do what you want to do and fewer feelings of guilt or shame. Letting go of mental clutter is just as significant as letting go of physical clutter.

> Striving for perfection is the greatest stopper there is. It's your excuse to yourself for not doing anything. Instead, strive for excellence, doing your best.
> – Sir Laurence Olivier

Don't wait to start your effort until the moment when everything is going exactly as you had planned. Make a plan for the times when you will make mistakes or end up disappointed. From now on, work toward excellence, not perfection.

Decision Making

Some clients ask me how other people handle a situation or what other people do with their clutter. I always wonder why they want to know what someone else does. Is it because they're looking for new ideas? Or is it to validate what they're already doing? Maybe it's because people like to be like others, to fit in.

Usually I say that it doesn't matter what other people do, because their circumstances are going to be different. No one is going to have the same space, configuration, furniture, storage, items, and financial state that you do. The best plan is for you to think about what will work optimally for you, given your space and financial limitations, along with the style you like and the way you use things.

> *The saddest summary of a life contains three descriptions: could have, might have, and should have. - Louis E. Boone*

The greatest challenge most people have with organizing is decision making, which is the key to letting go of clutter. Clutter accumulates because you have put off making decisions about it. I have seen clients who agonize over every decision. When you allow yourself to become so overwhelmed that you can't decide what to keep and where to put it, you allow your things to take over your life. You can spend so much time agonizing over the details that you miss out on the big picture, which is to live with what you value and enjoy what you have.

We have more choices today than ever. Having so many options, though, can make it hard to pick just one. Visiting a market, department store or warehouse outlet can turn into a complex decision-making event; overwhelmed by all the choices, you leave without making a purchase.

There are so many things that need your attention, how do you decide what to do? You are constantly resetting priorities, based on your energy level, skills, beliefs and experience.

Having criteria for making decisions will help you with both small and large projects. When you have a system to funnel decisions through, you can focus your energies on carrying out tasks.

Soliciting too many opinions will delay your decision. If you value other people's input, put a limit on how many people you will ask. You can develop a list of contacts to consult in different circumstances. For example, have three people whose counsel you will seek when you have to make financial decisions, three people whose taste in clothing you admire, three people whom you trust to know about technology, etc. By sticking to a predetermined number of advisors, you limit the input you get and allow yourself to make a well-informed decision. When you ask other people for suggestions, you need to consider what you like, what your budget is and how much room you have. Don't allow someone to talk you into a decision that doesn't feel right to you.

In order to start exercising your decision-making muscles, just do one thing. Take an action. It may feel uncomfortable at first, but it will get easier. Making a physical effort toward your goal will get you in the mental state to carry out the actions. Try making small decisions first, which you will build on over time.

Data Gathering

In 2009, the Oxford English Dictionary added "information fatigue" as a listing. Sheena Iyengar, author of *The Art of Choosing*, says people believe they want more information, but the result is all that information can cause them to become overwhelmed and unable to choose.

Academics who study decision science have found that when people have more information they tend to make poorer choices, which they later regret. In other cases, the overly thorough information-gathering process provides an excuse for not making a decision at all.

> ### Letting Go, Real Life:
>
> I worked with a client who wanted to buy a file cabinet. She read online everything she could find about file cabinets, drawer capacity and ball-bearing loads. She studied room layouts in catalogs and read reviews in consumer magazines. She checked buyers' reviews on store websites. All of these activities took hours of her time and kept her from making a decision for several weeks. After all her information gathering, she was still unable to choose a file cabinet.
>
> I asked her to narrow down her choices to five file cabinets, using the following criteria: size, color and price. Once she limited her choice, it was much easier for us to talk about the relative merits of each and within a half hour, she had chosen the file cabinet she really wanted
>
> There are so many ways to get information that you can spend all of your time reading about something instead of doing anything about it. Limiting your choices will make it easier for you to come up with a solution.

In your quest to find a product, you may do some research to find the item that meets your requirements. Exploring options when you consider a purchase can help you make an educated choice; however, if you continue to study alternatives, you will delay making a choice at all. If you know that you can spend hours researching and analyzing options, don't let that be your starting point. Before you begin your search, narrow down what you will look for and stick to those parameters.

Don't let information overload keep you from making a decision. Set a limit on how many samples you will get, bids you will solicit or opinions you will seek, for example, then decide to decide within a specific period of time. Keep your basic criteria straightforward and realize that there will be more than one "right" choice.

Crisis Mode

If you thrive on the adrenaline rush you get when you put things off until the last minute or you cram too much into your day, you might believe that there is no other way to live. In fact, when you create stress for yourself by manufacturing crises, you choose to make your life more complicated than it needs to be. Slowing down the pace of your life can cause you to get more done, not less.

Most people who routinely operate in crisis mode think that they are handling things well. It isn't until someone brings it to your attention that you recognize your own behavior. If you aren't ready to change the way you do things, you may cause yourself physical harm. Stress causes the body to secrete cortisol, a hormone linked with anxiety and agitation. Chronic stress can speed up the aging process and increase risk of heart disease and stroke; it can affect your memory as well.

> Follow effective action with quiet reflection. From the quiet reflection will come even more effective action.
> - Peter Drucker

Any of us can find ourselves in a situation where we have too much to do and not enough time to do it. The key is to decide what merits doing and what can be disregarded. If you only know how to operate in crisis mode, it will be difficult for you to think differently, especially if you are someone who waits until the last minute and gets a rush from the self-induced pressure.

Think about a day when you were so busy you didn't even stop to eat, yet you felt like you accomplished nothing. At the end of the day, you were left with the same list of things you started with. If this happens to you often, you may be over-scheduling yourself or doing things you could be delegating. You might be doing things that don't need to be done until a later date. Being energetic is good, but being frenzied is not.

Some people like to look busy because they think it makes them seem valuable. If you're not producing quality work, though, someone is bound to notice eventually. It's important to find a balance between being idle and being stressed, with the outcome of achieving your goals. Being busy and being productive are not the same.

If you are moving your objectives forward, accomplishing what you need to, then you are having a productive day. Filling your day with unimportant tasks causes you to be busy but doesn't leave time for things you need to do. Spending time searching for things can keep you busy, too, with the same result.

If you are going to break the habit of living in constant crisis, you need to make some changes to the way you think about time. Have a plan for handling situations before they twist out of control. Learn to tell the difference between what is truly important and what can wait. Ask yourself if it would be better to handle something immediately, before it becomes a crisis. Choose how much time you will invest in yourself each day, instead of allowing time to slip away from you.

You will benefit from checking your calendar regularly to make sure you are not scheduling yourself so tightly that you're unable to dedicate enough time to each task. Take 10 minutes at the end of each day to put everything away and plan for the next day. Create a sense of order and structure so you are able to experience smoother transitions and less hectic days.

Living Your Plan

If you're still struggling with where to start, ask yourself, "What part of my home or office is most important to me?" and focus on clearing the clutter from that area. Otherwise, start with the place that's bothering you the most. Consider how clearing out that space would help you. Then visualize what it will look like and how it will function when the clutter is gone.

Letting go of clutter doesn't mean you have to get rid of everything you own; it allows you to access what you value and enjoy it. When you identify what's not working for you, you can begin the process.

> **Letting go of clutter is a process, not an event**

Remember that, to be successful, you need to work at your plan regularly. Commit to spending just 10 minutes a day decluttering; it really will make a difference. Keep your goals in mind so that you can maintain your habits and prevent the clutter from returning.

When you feel frustrated or unmotivated, don't give up. Don't allow clutter to overcome you. You deserve to live a life free from unclear thoughts, excessive commitments and unneeded things. Having a trusted partner to help keep you focused is very useful. You can find an online community of people who are experiencing the same challenges as you.

You also might benefit from creating a life list. Different from a to-do list, a life list consists of the things you want to accomplish in life. It helps you figure out what is most meaningful to you.

Simply writing things down isn't going to make them happen; however, seeing your wishes on paper may prompt you to actually make them come true. View your list monthly and take small steps toward achieving your goals. You can update your list annually, crossing off the things that no longer appeal to you and adding new ones.

Get started by going to one of the Web sites where people post their life lists, such as 43 Things, My Life List or 2 Do Before I Die. You may be inspired by other people's posts, which range from finishing high school to growing an organic garden. Not surprisingly, getting organized appears on many people's lists.

You can let go of the clutter that holds you back. Take a small step every day and celebrate your success.

About Hoarding

People frequently ask me how someone can live with extreme clutter and not recognize it. Clutter generally takes some time to build up and when it becomes too much to deal with, the person learns to ignore it. After a while, he or she becomes accustomed to the way things are and doesn't recognize it for what it is. Although people living in chaos may have some awareness of the situation, they haven't accepted it and they live in a state of denial. Often, it is too painful for them to think about the situation.

True hoarders are unable to part with their accumulations. Some of them hoard animals, others hoard what looks like trash; all of them have serious issues that cause them to continue the behavior, regardless of health or sanitary conditions.

If you believe that someone you know is a hoarder, you need to understand that he or she may not accept assistance. When they do agree to get help, hoarders can be extremely difficult to work with. The biggest mistake you can make is to clear out a space without getting the person to agree with the decision. Hoarders have a strong attachment to their things and need help to determine what can be discarded.

Hoarders will not change their behavior unless they are really motivated to live differently and are given the appropriate tools to do so. They cannot help themselves; they need guidance, direction and support. If you are a hoarder, you can benefit from the services of a professional organizer, in combination with therapy.

For more information about hoarding, consult the Institute for Challenging Disorganization (ICD), formerly known as The National Study Group on Chronic Disorganization (NSGCD).

Resources

Organized by Marcie blog
www.organizedbymarcie.blogspot.com

National Association of Professional Organizers
www.napo.net

Institute for Challenging Disorganization
www.challengingdisorganization.org

National Do Not Call registry
www.ftc.gov/donotcall

Mail Preference Service
www.dmachoice.org

Stop credit card solicitations
www.optoutprescreen.com

Stop phone book delivery
www.yellowpagesgoesgreen.org

Lifehacker
http://lifehacker.com

Merlin Mann's 43 folders
www.43folders.com

Linda Stone
http://lindastone.net

Jeff Yeager
www.ultimatecheapskate.com

Life lists
www.43things.com
www.mylifelist.org
www.2dobeforeidie.org

Bibliography

Allen, David. *Getting Things Done: The Art of Stress-Free Productivity*

Ariely, Dan. *Predictably Irrational: The Hidden Forces That Shape Our Decisions*

Benson, April Lane. *To Buy or Not to Buy: Why We Overshop and How to Stop*

Eisenberg, Lee. *Shoptimism: Why the American Consumer Will Keep on Buying No Matter What*

Iyengar, Sheena. *The Art of Choosing*

Jaggar, Louisa and Don Williams. *Saving Stuff: How to Care for and Preserve Your Collectibles, Heirlooms, and Other Prized Possessions*

Morgenstern, Julie. *Organizing from the Inside Out: The Foolproof System For Organizing Your Home, Your Office and Your Life*

Singletary, Michelle. *The Power to Prosper: 21 Days to Financial Freedom*

Underhill, Paco. *Why We Buy: The Science of Shopping*

Ury, William. *The Power Of A Positive No: Save The Deal Save The Relationship and Still Say No*

Walsh, Peter. *It's All Too Much: An Easy Plan for Living a Richer Life with Less Stuff*

Winston, Stephanie. *The Organized Executive: A Program for Productivity--New Ways to Manage Time, Paper, People, and the Digital Office*

Acknowledgements

I am truly indebted to Stephanie Winston, who wrote *The Organized Executive*. If I had not read her book many years ago, I never would have known that the work I enjoy so much could become my career.

I am grateful for everyone who believed in this project, including Dan Janal of PRLeads, my fearless PR leader; Laura Levengard of StarPower Fitness, my accountability partner and cheering section; Mui Chao of Simply Mui Photography, my saintly photographer and encouragement manager; and Chris Davis, who helped me maintain my sense of humor along with my timeline. I also am thankful for Dr. Roget, who created my trusted thesaurus.

Most importantly, I appreciate all of the people who participate in my seminars and work with me individually. I have learned so much from you and you continue to inspire me.

Marcie Speaks To You

Marcie Lovett keeps audiences engaged by providing pertinent examples and exceptionally helpful methods for letting go of the clutter in your life. Her friendly, informative and entertaining presentation style motivates you to get your projects started.

To have Marcie speak to your group or conduct a workshop, email sales@organizedbymarcie.com.

About the Author

Marcie Lovett is a Professional Organizer and Productivity Consultant. As owner of **_Organized by Marcie_**™, she has helped hundreds of people save time and money by letting go of what they don't need and finding room for what they value. She coaches clients on productivity and goal setting and offers seminars and training for businesses, schools, clubs and other groups. She has been featured in a number of publications and on radio and TV programs.

Marcie graduated from the University of Maryland, School of Education, and attended Pepperdine University for graduate work in Business Administration. She is a Golden Circle member of the National Association of Professional Organizers (NAPO). Prior to starting her own business, she had many years of experience assisting people with their organizational needs at home and in healthcare, finance and non-profit settings.

Marcie lives in the Washington, DC area and enjoys digging in her garden when she is not working with clients, writing or teaching people how to let go of clutter.

Made in the USA
Charleston, SC
02 November 2012